About the Author

DaVida Rowley is a Brooklyn, New York native with a passion for uplifting others through her personal testimony of rising above the odds to achieve success. Despite losing her mother to drug addiction at the age 11, she maintained a strong desire for excellence and a will to succeed. After graduating as valedictorian of her elementary school, she went on to maintain good grades in High School.

In her senior year of High School, DaVida became pregnant with her son. Instead of seeing this as an obstacle, she became even more motivated. She not only graduated High School on time but earned three scholarships and began studying at Hunter College while her son was just a few weeks old.

Through the grace of God, she earned a degree in Sociology and has enjoyed a fulfilling career in Social Services for the past decade. Her personal mission is to help people create the lives they desire. To this end, DaVida has helped hundreds of individuals take steps towards self-improvement both professionally and personally. She enjoys traveling to new islands, reading, and spending time with her amazing teenage son, Katrell. She is a proud Christian who always seeks to be an example of the love, grace, and mercy of God.

Dedication

For my son Katrell Price:

You are the light of my life. You are the most amazing soul I know. I am blessed beyond measure because of your existence. May God grant you peace all the days of your life. Remember to keep God first and pursue excellence always.

With Love,
Mom

Introduction

*Why do we only **rest** in peace?*
*Why can't we **live** in peace too?*

God's word says that his plans are to prosper us and not harm us (Jeremiah 29:11). So, why are so many of us not living prosperous lives? I'm not talking about having money or material things. That's the world's definition. The kind of prosperity I'm talking about is **inner peace.** That is what God wants us to have. You see, God did not create us to be miserable, stressed, and unhappy. God created us for something bigger, something better. He is waiting patiently for the day when we discover that **unless we have inner peace, nothing else matters.**

Just think about yourself for a moment. Are there times when you allow people and circumstances to threaten your peace? Do you sometimes feel like things just aren't the way you want them to be? Are you lacking peace within yourself? Do you feel like you could be doing more and being more?

A few years ago, I would have answered yes to all the questions I just asked you. Now listen, my life at the time was not necessarily bad. I was blessed with a growing career, an amazing son, a long-term relationship, and a lifestyle that allowed me to do what I love most — travel. It was good on the outside. But I still wasn't happy on the inside. My spirit was not at peace, until **I decided to do something about it**!

It all started when I made a choice to let go of the three things that were affecting my peace the most: my job, my home, and my relationship. I was working at a job with toxic people who drained my spirit, I was in a miserable relationship with my partner of ten years, and I had just moved into a neighborhood in an unfamiliar town that brought me anxiety. I began to feel in my spirit that there was time for a major change. So within the span of three months, I let them all go. One. By. One. I quit the job, ended the relationship, and then moved out of the apartment. As scary as this process was, I trusted that God would not only see me through it, but that there would be victory on the other side. I spent the next few months getting clear with myself about what I wanted out of life, releasing the baggage of my past, and making choices that served my spirit and the vision God had for my life. After releasing these things, I was able to reestablish myself as the powerful being God created me to be and make the decisions necessary to create a sense of harmony within. **I found my inner peace**. And it was the best feeling in the world.

So, my good news to you is this: there is something you can do about it too! You don't have to be stuck or live an unhappy life or feel like your spirit isn't at peace. Through this book, you will have 40 different affirmations, prayers, and actions you can use to begin creating the peaceful life you deserve. These strategies address real-life struggles that many of us face. If your desire is strong enough and you are committed to the process, I have no doubt that you'll be able to find the peace you've been searching for.

My hope is that with each chapter you will be able to*:*

- Come to your own understanding and realizations about what's affecting your inner peace
- Claim victory over it through **affirmation**
- Release it to God through **prayer**
- Make a change through **action**

Before you begin reading, a quick note about affirmations:

In the affirmations section of each chapter, you will find powerful declarative statements. These statements are written in the first person, "I' form, so you can speak them over yourself. When you speak them with conviction and authority, they truly have the power to shift and move things in your life. Read them to yourself several times if you need to.

A Prayer for You

Dear God,

Please bless the person reading this book. I pray that as they begin this journey, they will do so with a clear mind and a willing heart. Lord, as they read each chapter, let the words speak life over them. Let the words touch their minds and spirits in a way that they may be inspired to make a change for the better. Help them to know that you have great plans for their lives and you have not forgotten about them. Remind them that they are loved and cared for by you.

I declare Lord that through this book, they will have victory over the things that threaten their peace. They will gain the strength to **LET GO** of things that need to be released, the willpower to **STOP** doing the things that don't serve them, the energy to **FOCUS** on the things that deserve their attention, a sound mind to **LEARN** the things that will help them to have peace, the commitment to **BE** who they need to be in order to have the life they desire, the tenacity to **KEEP** hold of the things that will enable them to maintain a peaceful life, and the courage to **OWN** the things that will help them stand in their power.

In the name of Jesus, I lift this prayer. *Amen.*

CONTENTS

CONTENTS

Part V — What to Be

Part VI — What to Keep

Part VII — What to Own

PART I

...

What to Let Go

CHAPTER ONE

Let Go of People, Places, and Things that Don't Serve You

"Your next blessing depends on what you leave behind."
–UNKNOWN

"It is the LORD who goes before you. He will be with you; he will not leave you or forsake you. Do not fear or be dismayed."
—DEUTERONOMY 31:8

▲ Affirmation ▲

I do not have to stay in a place where I am not respected, valued, or nurtured. There are better places for me. I do not have to stay with a person who does not respect, value, or nurture me. There is a better person for me. I do not have to keep doing the same things that get me nowhere. There are better things for me to do. I will not pretend that I don't know when someone, something or some place is not in my best interest. I am well aware of the people, places, and things that do and don't serve me. I will be honest with myself and have the courage to walk away from those things that seek to keep me down and keep me stuck.

I AM NOT A SLAVE.

Why would I stay in a *place* that breaks my spirit? Why would I stay with a *person* that breaks my spirit? Why would I do *things* that don't serve my spirit?

I have choices. I can do anything that I choose. ANYTHING. That is why God gave me free will. He wants me to create a life that is pleasing to him and fulfilling to my soul.

I know that walking away is not easy. But there is *freedom* on the other side of my goodbye. There is *hope* on the other side of my goodbye. There is *abundance* on the other side of my goodbye. I will make a choice that honors me. I will put myself first. I will say no to what I don't want, in order to say yes to what I do want. I will use all the strength I have to say... Goodbye!

▲ Prayer ▲

Lord, saying Goodbye is hard. There are stories and emotions attached to people, places, and things that can have me stuck. There are good stories and bad stories, but stories nevertheless. There are deep connections to people, places, and things. Although the bad parts may outweigh the good parts Lord, I sometimes want to hold on to the good just a little bit longer. Give me the strength Lord to let go. Give me the courage to choose what is best for me even if that means saying goodbye.

There are real challenges Lord that come with saying goodbye: financial challenges, emotional challenges, physical challenges. But those challenges don't compare to the freedom, peace, and joy that you have promised me. I know you wouldn't tell me to leave something unless there was something better. You are not a "set me up" God. You don't have any tricks up your sleeve. You simply want to see me at my best and sometimes that means letting go of the wrong people, places, and things, so that my hands can be free to hold all the great things you have for me.

Lord, there may come a time when I let go of something and want to backtrack. I may want to pick up the phone and call someone who isn't good for me. Help me stand firm. I may want to go back to the place you delivered me from. Help me to stand firm. I may want to do things I used to do that didn't serve me well. Help me to stand firm. Stay with me Lord. In the name of Jesus, I lift this prayer. **Amen.**

▲ Action ▲

Check-in with yourself

What people, places, and things are causing me to not have the peace I want?

Make a choice

Today I choose to let go of the people, places, and things that don't serve me because I want to be free to receive the things God has for me.

Act on your choice

≈ If you're living or working in a place that doesn't bring you peace, plan to transition out. Always put some funds aside in case you need to leave a situation.

≈ If you're in a relationship that doesn't fulfill you, gain the courage to walk away. Don't let anything be an excuse (including children or shared property).

≈ Clean up the contacts in your phone. If there are people who bring you more harm than good, they should be deleted or blocked.

CHAPTER TWO

Let Go of the Past

"The past is a place of reference, not a place of residence."
—WILLIE JOLLEY

"Forget the former things; do not dwell on the past. See, I am doing a new thing! Now it springs up; do you not perceive it?"
—ISAIAH 43:18-19

▲ Affirmation ▲

I am not a slave to my past. I will not be held hostage by it. Yes, there may be things that I am not proud of, but that doesn't make me less worthy. There are things that have been done to me: painful things, hurtful things, damaging things. But I declare that those things are washed away. I release the need to hold on to what was done to me. What happened, whether good or bad, cannot be undone. I will not get so stuck dwelling on who was at fault or on things I could have and should have done. I will accept that I did what I could with the knowledge and tools I had at that time. I choose to appreciate the lessons and experiences while moving forward with a fresh perspective.

I know that there is more that God wants to do, in spite of my shortcomings. God knew that I would make mistakes, but he also knew that I would have the strength to recover from those mistakes and be better. The fact that I am still here means God wants me to move on and be better. Today is a new day! Yesterday is gone. I will embrace all that there is right here and now. God is a God of the present. I will meet him right here and now; and together we will do great things.

▲ Prayer ▲

Lord, I don't want to be a prisoner of my past anymore. Please help me to let go of past experiences that seek to weigh me down. Remove from me the need to obsess over what I could and should have done. I trust that whatever you have given me to experience up until this point was meant for my good. No matter what it may look like to others Lord, I know that you know the very best of me. Help me to understand the things I need to learn from my past. I know that you have set up certain situations for me to receive information, or a lesson, or an understanding that I can use in my future endeavors. Help me to take heed to those lessons so that I may be a better me.

I release to you my need to place blame on myself or others for choices that have been made, mistakes that have been made, things that have been done. Although folks may have caused me hurt, I need to have peace with it. Although there may be things in my past that are not in line with being my best self, I ask that you help me to disconnect what I have done or experienced in the past from who I am. I know that despite it all, I am still loved by you. In the name of Jesus, I lift this prayer. ***Amen.***

▲ Action ▲

Check-in with yourself

What do I need to let go of from my past? Abandonment, hurt, pain, disappointment, regret, guilt? Certain people? Certain situations?

Make a choice

Today I choose to let go of my past because it has no power and I deserve to be free.

Act on your choice

≈ Write a letter to the person(s) who have caused you hurt and pain. You don't have to send it to them unless you want to. Just simply releasing it can bring you peace. If the space allows, have a conversation with the person.

≈ Seek therapy if needed. Don't be afraid or ashamed. It's a sign of courage and a commitment to be your best self.

CHAPTER THREE

Let Go of What Others Think of You

"Care about other people's approval, and you will always be their prisoner."
—LAO TZU

"Am I now trying to win the approval of human beings, or of God? Or am I trying to please people? If I were still trying to please people, I would not be a servant of Christ."
—GALATIANS 1:10

▲ Affirmation ▲

I will not be imprisoned by the thoughts and opinions of others or allow my self-worth to be dictated by society. I know who I am to God and I know who he has called me to be. God made me in **his** image; not the image of society, not the image of a celebrity, not the image of my parents, not the image of my partner, not the image of my friends. In. God's. Image. And if God is for me, who can be against me? What others think of me is irrelevant. Society can create all the values it wants, that has nothing to do with what God has told me about who I am.

I don't have to seek approval from anyone. I have full authority to be me, unapologetically. I may not have the body I want, I may not have the things I want, I may not have accomplished everything there is to accomplish yet. It doesn't matter. **I am still complete and perfect just the way I am.**

My uniqueness does not have to be accepted by everyone. I don't need anyone to understand or agree that my ideas and decisions sound good. Even if I am the only one who believes in me, that will be enough. God gave me a vision and his approval is all I need.

The opinions of others cannot make or break me. This is **my** life, not theirs. God has not given anyone commandment over who I am, what I am worth, and what I can and cannot do. If there are people who have a negative opinion of me, that is only a reflection of them, not me. I can pray for them from a distance, but I dare not let their ill ways define me.

When God made me, it was *after* the amazing sunsets and sunrises, after the powerful oceans and rivers. God looked at all of this and still he knew the world needed one, and only one, of me. Surely, there is power and amazement in me too. I see myself the way God sees me. What others cannot see is no fault of mine. When I look in the mirror, I see nothing but greatness. There is only perfection running through my veins. God doesn't make anything less than perfect. I will embrace my uniqueness. I will embrace my flaws. I will embrace my mistakes. I will embrace **every** part of me. I believe if God woke me up then there is still a need for me. What I have, the world did not give to me and it cannot take it away. My worth comes from God and God alone.

▲ Prayer ▲

Lord, thank you for making me in *your* image. Thank you that even my flaws are perfect in your sight. You knew me even before I existed in my mother's womb. You created me to be a unique force in this world. Therefore, let me not be concerned with what others think. People will always have opinions, but you know me at my core. You know the very best parts of me. Help me to focus on you.

God, your approval is all I need. All that matters is what you think of me. And if you are for me God, who can be against me? Lord, when people don't support me or affirm me, show me how to move ahead anyway. The truth is Lord, that the vision you have given me is special to me. If you wanted others to see it, you would have given them the vision too. Let me stand firm on what you have told me about me.

Lord, if I begin to get wrapped up in what others think, bring my mind back to who I am. Remind me, oh God, that when it's all over, it will be **you** who says, "well done", not anyone else. Please let my worth rest only in you. In the name of Jesus, I lift this prayer. ***Amen.***

▲ Action ▲

Check-in with yourself

What am I not doing because I'm worried about what other people think? What am I not doing because I'm waiting for other people's approval and support?

Make a choice

Today I choose to let go of needing other people's approval and what other people think of me because all that matters is what God thinks of me.

Act on your choice

≈ Do whatever you feel is in your heart to do without considering anyone else's opinion. Wear what you want to wear, speak how you want to speak, think what you want to think. **Just be you!**

≈ Don't wait for anyone to agree in order to act on your idea. Make a plan and then do it!

CHAPTER FOUR

Let Go of the Need to Know Everything

"The only true wisdom is in knowing you know nothing."

—SOCRATES

"Trust in the LORD with all your heart and lean not on your own understanding."

—PROVERBS 3:5

▲ Affirmation ▲

I cannot afford to let what I don't know get in the way of moving forward with the things I am seeking to accomplish. As I pursue greatness, everything won't be 100% clear all the time. But if my intentions are clear, God will provide me the knowledge I need.

There are things simply not meant for me to know right now. There may even be things that I will never know. However, I will not get fixated on trying to figure everything out. I am not an all-knowing being. Sometimes, my intuition will be all that I have. It was placed there for a reason. My intuition is like the spirit of God within me trying to get me to feel things that I may not be 100% privy to at that moment.

When my mind starts to wonder what it is, many times it isn't something in the grasp of my mind at that time. I will be okay with that. I do not need to know everything. Besides, if I knew everything it might take the fun out of life. I may have to just trust my gut and keep it moving.

▲ Prayer ▲

Lord thank you for the gift of discernment. Thank you for placing the Holy Spirit inside of me to give me senses beyond my own capabilities. Build up in me a stronger reception to it so that I know how to discern when you are seeking to keep me from something that is *not* in my best interest or push me towards something that *is* for my best interest.

As I seek to pursue my endeavors, I pray that you help me to be okay with not knowing all the details. Allow me to move on in spite of this, trusting that what you have for me will not miss me. If I begin to question things, stop me in my tracks. I don't need to know every detail. I just need to know that you have my best interest at heart and you won't let me fail.

I know that many times when I don't know something, you are protecting me from my own self. If I knew everything, there are decisions that I might not make; ones that are ultimately good for me. If I knew everything, I might not enjoy the experience as much. So, I trust that you will show me whatever you need me to know. In the name of Jesus, I lift this prayer. ***Amen***.

▲ Action ▲

Check-in with yourself

Do I normally trust my intuition or do I have to wait for every detail before moving? How good am I at discerning what my spirit is trying to tell me?

Make a choice

Today I choose to let go of the need to know everything and trust my intuition because it comes from God.

Act on your choice

≈ The next time you get that gut feeling about something, follow it. Don't hesitate or start overthinking.

≈ Stay in touch with your spirit when you are making decisions about people or things. Unlike your mind that can lead you astray, the spirit never lies.

PART II

. . .

What to Stop Doing

CHAPTER FIVE

Stop Placing Limits on God

"We ought not to limit God where He has not limited Himself."

— JONATHAN EDWARDS

"I am the Lord, the God of all mankind. Is anything too hard for me?"
—JEREMIAH 32:27

▲ Affirmation ▲

I will not get amnesia about who God is. He has done wonders for me many times and he will do many more. I dare not forget how powerful capable, and limitless he is. There are things that I cannot even begin to imagine that God can do. I have not seen the depth of all there is to know about God. His power is infinite. It knows no bounds. There is nothing that God cannot do.

Many people may look at my past or at who I am and think there are things that simply cannot be done with me. But I know differently. I know that God can do great things through me because he has already done so. He is not concerned with any challenges I may have. God specializes in challenges. That is where he does his best work.

Because of God's power I can rest assured that I will be able to tackle any situation. I have to remember that I am not walking alone. God is with me. He has prepared a plan long before my situation was a situation. Whatever I cannot do on my own accord, he can. He will stand in the gap. He will make me strong when I am weak. He will provide me answers when I don't have the answers. He will make clear what seems unclear. All that I need, God is able to do.

▲ Prayer ▲

Lord, I stand in reverence and awe of just how great and powerful you are. You have already shown me what you are capable of. Every time I open my eyes I am reminded of your power. Every time I move, I am reminded of your power. It is *your* spirit dwelling within me that allows me to function. Let me not forget that because you live in me not only are *you* powerful, but I am too.

In tough situations, Lord let me not be afraid because you have already worked it out. As long as I depend on you, the victory will be won. Let me rely on your power and your strength over my own. You've already considered every possibility, every angle, every pitfall. You see things I cannot see. I will trust in you more than my own self. I know if I place something in your hands it will not return empty.

Lord help me to remove the limitations that I have placed on you. There are times oh Lord, that I forget that I should not put you in the same box that I place myself. I think only of the difficulty of the situation. But your word says there is *nothing* that is too hard for you. Let this be on my mind and in my spirit always. In the name of Jesus, I lift this prayer. ***Amen.***

▲ Action ▲

Check-in with yourself

In what situations has God shown me his power? Do I only have faith about some things and not others?

Make a choice

Today I choose to stop placing limits on God because there is nothing he cannot do.

Act on your choice

≈ The next time you encounter a tough situation, remind yourself that God has done it before and he will do it again.

≈ Stop treating God like he's human and placing him in a box. He is not limited by the things you are. Don't treat God like a regular 'ol person.

CHAPTER SIX

Stop Trying to Do Too Much

"You can do anything, if you stop trying to do everything."

—OLIVER EMBERTON

"Come to me, all you who are weary and burdened, and I will give you rest. Take my yoke upon you and learn from me, for I am gentle and humble in heart, and you will find rest for your souls. For my yoke is easy and my burden is light."

—MATTHEW 11:28-30

▲ Affirmation ▲

I am not in a race or competition with anyone to see how quickly I can get things done or how many things I can do. Instead, I am in the marathon of my life. I am in this for the long haul, so there is no need to rush. I will build my legacy brick by brick.

Taking on too much at one time is not only unrealistic, but it is also unhealthy for me. Even if I have a high threshold of how much activity I can handle at once, I may be causing mental and physical damage to myself that isn't always apparent at the time. What good will I be to myself or others if I wear myself down?

Overloading myself with work or activities does not make me productive. Pacing myself and tackling things one-by-one, is the best way for me to achieve longevity. I don't need to take on a bunch of different things just to show people that I'm working or make myself feel good. I already know what I am capable of.

Truthfully, there are only so many things that I can do well at once. Instead of doing many things *kind of well*, I would be better off doing a few things very well. My reputation for quality over quantity is what will shine through.

▲ Prayer ▲

Lord thank you for the abilities you've given me to accomplish many things at once. Thank you for my energy and ambition. I know that these are ultimately gifts, but I also know that if my gifts are not treasured and used accordingly, they will not be able to serve me well.

Help me to take a step back when I am doing too much, Lord. Don't let me overwork myself to the point that my mental space or even my health can be at risk. I pray that if you sense I could be causing myself more harm than good by focusing on too much at once, you will give me a nudge to slow it down.

I want to be here to enjoy the fruits of my labor Lord. I want to be effective in all that I do. I want to be productive and not just busy. Don't allow me to focus just on showing that I can produce a lot of results. Help me to take the time I need to ensure what I am doing is effective. Lord, show me how to find the balance. In the name of Jesus, I lift this prayer. **Amen**.

▲ Action ▲

Check-in with yourself

Am I trying to do too much at one time? What point am I trying to prove? What am I going to lose out on if I don't do everything at the same time?

Make a choice

Today I choose to stop trying to do too much and focus on building little by little because I realize that overloading myself is unhealthy.

Act on your choice

≈ Look at your to do list or calendar and eliminate the things that seem unnecessary.

≈ Give yourself a limit of how many things you will take on at one time. Don't commit to doing things if you don't have the capacity.

≈ Take a step back if you feel yourself getting overwhelmed by too many things. Remember the work isn't going anywhere.

CHAPTER SEVEN

Stop Holding on to Anger and Frustration

"For every minute you remain angry, you give up sixty seconds of peace of mind."
—RALPH WALDO EMERSON

"Refrain from anger and turn from wrath; do not fret—it leads only to evil."
—PSALMS 37:8

▲ Affirmation ▲

Everything will not go my way all the time. People will do things that I don't agree with, or things that hurt me or upset me. I may get frustrated with a particular situation. There is no escaping this. Feeling frustrated and angry is a normal part of life. But if I stay frustrated and angry, that is a choice. It's how I deal with the situation that sets me apart and determines if I will have peace.

It does not make sense for me to hold on to anger and frustration for a long time; or even a little time. There is little good that can come from it. Unless it's going to push me to do better or be better, I might as well let it go. Most of the time, it's just not worth it.

Instead of holding onto anger or frustration, I will resolve the matter at hand with those involved. A simple conversation may be what's needed. A change in approach may be what's needed. Thinking through a solution may be what's needed. Whatever it is, I will seek to resolve the matter in a way that yields a positive result rather than sulk and be bitter about it. You see *I* hold the power. And staying angry and frustrated is not a power move.

▲ Prayer ▲

Lord free me from any anger and frustration that may be stirring within me. I release to you the situation with hope and expectancy for a resolution. Help me to see that anger is never the solution. If there is *something* I am upset about I can change it. If I can't, then I can accept it peacefully. If there is *someone* I am upset with I can change it. If I can't, then I can accept it peacefully. Remind me oh God that being angry is always a lose-lose situation.

Forgive me for the times Lord when I let my anger overtake me. I know that your word says *be slow to anger* but it can be hard sometimes Lord. Please have patience with me as I learn how to deal with things in a different way. Show me how to communicate when I'm frustrated and angry. Help me to remain calm. Help me to experience the frustration and anger, make a choice, and then move on. Don't let me get stuck in it oh Lord. Thank you for allowing me to grow through difficult experiences. I know that I am not at my best if I allow anger to control me. Help me to be my best. In the name of Jesus, I lift this prayer. ***Amen***.

▲ Action ▲

Check-in with yourself

Am I quick to get over things or do I let things continue to simmer? What particular situations or people seem to get me angry? Do I let my emotions get out of control?

Make a choice

Today I choose to stop holding onto anger and frustration because it creates a lose-lose situation.

Act on your choice

≈ If you're in a disagreement, especially with someone you care about, take a moment to think before reacting. Always approach it from a place of love and not anger.

≈ Try to focus on the solution and not the emotion. Remember, it is not about who is wrong or right, it is about peace.

≈ Channel your frustration into change. Whatever you are frustrated about, it is probably worth thinking about how not to get to that place again.

CHAPTER EIGHT

Stop Feeling Entitled

"When gratitude replaces entitlement, things come to us easier and more abundantly."
—UNKNOWN

"We can say these things because of our faith in God through Christ. We know we are not able in ourselves to do any of this work. God makes us able to do these things."
—2 CORINTHIANS 3:4-5

▲ Affirmation ▲

God doesn't owe me anything. Everything he blesses me with is out of his love for me. When I wake up, I breathe, I move and function - that is all God, 100%. Not me. I am not owed another day, but I am given another day because God loves me like that. I am not going to walk around as though I am entitled to things. Everything I have and everything I am is a blessing from God.

I will not carry a sense of entitlement with those I love and care about either. They may love me, but they are in my life by choice. People do not have to do things in the way that I want or expect. In fact, they don't have to do anything at all. We are all different. We all have had different experiences and we all make different choices. Just because I may have a certain threshold or tolerance for something doesn't mean that other people will. Just because I can do something a particular way doesn't mean that other people will. Just because I go above and beyond in certain situations, doesn't mean other people have to. We are not all the same. If we were, life would be a lot less interesting.

When things don't go my way, I will not resort to childish ways by shaming others and making them feel bad for what they didn't do. Justifying my entitlement with past experiences doesn't make it right either. Even if I don't feel comfortable or agree with another person's choice, I am mature enough to allow people the space to be whoever and whatever they want to be. I anticipate that it won't be like me. That is not a negative thing. **Everything is not always about me.**

▲ Prayer ▲

Lord, help me to stay out of feelings and drop the sense of entitlement to people and things. Remind me that you created all of us in your image, uniquely. No two of us are the same. You gave us different experiences and viewpoints so that we could enjoy the diversity of one another. God, what would life be if you stopped being imaginative and made us into simple duplications of one another? I don't even want to know. Thank you for your creativity. What a mind you have!

Please forgive me oh Lord for those times when I acted like a child, pouting and shutting people out because they didn't do something I wanted or what I would have done. Forgive me for my inability to be mature in every moment. Allow me the space to try and be better with this. Teach me Lord, how to separate another person's choice or way of being from myself. The truth is this Lord; what they do and say, and what they choose has nothing to do with me personally. Help me to remember this. In the name of Jesus, I lift this prayer. *Amen*.

▲ Action ▲

Check-in with yourself

Do I have expectations that people will make the same choices that I would make? Do I think that things will automatically happen the way that I want and get upset if they don't?

Make a choice

Today I choose to stop feeling entitled because no one owes me anything.

Act on your choice

≈ The next time you encounter a situation where someone does not do something the way you would have chosen, remind yourself that we are all different. Appreciate the differences.

≈ Don't get angry with someone because they either choose to do something or not do something. People have a right to make their own choices.

CHAPTER NINE

Stop Trying to Do Everything Alone

"If you want to go fast, go alone. If you want to go far, go together."
—AFRICAN PROVERB

"Two are better than one, because they have a good reward for their toil. For if they fall, one will lift up his fellow. But woe to him who is alone when he falls and has not another to lift him up!"
—ECCLESIASTES 4:9-10

▲ Affirmation ▲

I might be strong and powerful, but that doesn't mean I can do everything on my own. There will be times that I have to rely on others for something. It's a part of life. Even if I've had bad experiences by depending on others, I will still seek out help when I need it. As long as I am not using folks, it's okay to ask. If I don't have people that I can depend on, that may be something for me to reflect on. I need to have strong, dependable folks around me in order to achieve the vision God has for my life. I cannot do it all alone. There will be someone with information that I need, someone with a connection that I need, someone with a resource that I need. These things are inevitable. **I. NEED. PEOPLE.** And they need me too. And that's okay.

Forget all the talk about being "self-made". There will always be more power in numbers. I don't need to win an award for doing everything on my own. I'm not proving a point to anyone but God. He is depending on me to put my pride aside and demonstrate that I can not only do great things, but I can do great things alongside others. I am eager to receive the knowledge of others and I am eager to share my own. I am eager for the skills of others and I am eager to share my own. I am eager for the energy that others bring, and I am eager to share with them my energy. Wanting to do everything alone is selfish. There are people who can benefit from my dopeness, from the way my mind works and from my spirit.

▲ Prayer ▲

Lord how amazing is it that you created so many great individuals for me to build and grow with? I can't imagine Lord how life would be if you left me to do everything on my own. Everything I have and everything I am is because someone came before me, because many others came before me and together they made things happen so that I could be here right now. If my mother hadn't worked with my father, Lord I wouldn't be here. If my grandfather hadn't worked with my grandmother, Lord I wouldn't be here. If all of my ancestors who endured so much didn't work together to create a better life for me, Lord I wouldn't be here. You created us to work together because we are so much stronger that way.

Forgive me Lord for thinking that I can do everything on my own. Forgive me for being selfish by not sharing myself with others. Help me to put aside my pride and leave any negative experiences I may have had with others behind. I know that not only I can benefit from others but they can also benefit from the amazing things that happen when we come together to support one another. Lord you made us to depend on each other. Someone was part of every good thing that has happened to me. Though it may have felt like I was on my own at times, I wasn't. I couldn't have done it alone. Teach me to fight through the urge to try to do things on my own. Help me to be okay with depending on others. In the name of Jesus, I lift this prayer. *Amen.*

▲ Action ▲

Check-in with yourself

Am I always trying to do something on my own? Do I let bad past experiences with reliability stop me from asking for help? Do I carry a "self-made" mentality?

Make a choice

Today I choose to stop trying to do everything alone because we are always stronger together and reliable people do exist.

Act on your choice

≈ Don't assume everyone is unreliable because you've had a few bad experiences.

≈ Connect with people who can help you achieve your vision. Build a reciprocal relationship where you are each benefiting one another.

≈ Drop the "self-made" talk. No one makes it by themselves. We all need people on the journey.

CHAPTER TEN

Stop Trying to Be Perfect

"There is no need to be perfect to inspire others. Let people get inspired by how you deal with your imperfections."
— ZIAD K. ABBDELNOUR

"Not that I have already obtained this or am already perfect, but I press on to make it my own, because Christ Jesus has made me his own."
—PHILIPPIANS 3:12

▲ Affirmation ▲

I am not in a competition to see how perfect I can be. Aiming to be the best I can be is important but obsessing over perfection is unhealthy. No one on this planet is "perfect". We all have flaws and things that we can improve. Trying to be perfect is not only unrealistic, it is exhausting. Overthinking what to say, what to do, how to act, how to look, when to say something, or how to do something takes a lot. And it's unnecessary.

I. AM. ENOUGH.

I don't have to do something a certain way. I can mess up and still be "perfect" in my own right. And I'm not going to allow society to make me feel as though I'm not. Society doesn't run my life, I do. Well actually, God does. And I know he thinks the best of me. My worthiness is not defined by anything outside of me.

Chasing perfection will have me tired and worn out. I won't have the energy to do all the great things I want to do. If my business idea isn't 100% perfect, I can try it anyway. If my outfit isn't 100% perfect, I can go out anyway. If I didn't say exactly what I wanted to say, I still did good. IT IS OKAY! I don't have to be so hard on myself. I refuse to treat myself like a punching bag, beating myself up for not being perfect. I have to trust and believe that I did the best I could at that time and keep it moving. If anything, there will be another time. Seriously, it's not that deep. I commit to lightening up a little, to giving myself space to not be perfect, to knowing that no matter what I say or do, even if I "mess up" a million times I am still amazing!

▲ Prayer ▲

Lord free me from the unnecessary need to be perfect all the time. I am thankful that when you look at me, you see nothing but perfection despite my flaws. Help me to resist getting too caught up in the details in a way that is not healthy for me. I want to be able to move forward even when things are not perfect Lord. God, the truth is that if I'm trying to be perfect then I am essentially cutting you out of the picture. There are times when I need to rely on your strength and not mine, on your ideas and not mine, on your ways and not mine. You made me imperfectly perfect so that I would still need you and others around me.

There are lessons in imperfection Lord. Help me to learn them. There are blessings in imperfection Lord, help me to receive them. I learn new things about myself when things don't go perfectly. I learn new things about others. Most importantly, I learn new things about you Lord. Open my mind so that I see that I don't need to get everything right. I don't have to know everything. Help me to be okay with this and to move forward in spite of it. In the name of Jesus, I lift this prayer. *Amen.*

▲ Action ▲

Check-in with yourself

Do I go above and beyond trying to be perfect? Have I missed out on opportunities because everything wasn't perfect? Do I beat myself up over the smallest mistakes?

Make a choice

Today I choose to stop trying to be perfect because I am already amazing just the way I am.

Act on your choice

≈ Accept that being perfect is an illusion. You will mess up. You won't always have it together and you don't need to.

≈ The next time you don't look perfect, go out anyway. The next time you do something imperfectly, celebrate anyway. Move through the imperfection. You can still win in spite of it.

PART III

. . .

What to Focus On

CHAPTER ELEVEN

Focus on What You Can Control

"Between stimulus and response there is a space. In that space is our power to choose our response. In our response lies our growth and our freedom."

—VIKTOR FRANKL

"Rise up; this matter is in your hands. We will support you, so take courage and do it."

—EZRA 10:4

▲ Affirmation ▲

I simply cannot have control over everything that happens in my life. Sometimes I am at the mercy of other people. Other times, situations just may not go as planned. In these times, my focus should not be on what I cannot control but instead on what I *can* do. By focusing on what I can do, I spend my energy wisely. When I get wrapped up in what I can't control, I begin to lose my power.

"I cannot always control what happens to me, but I can choose how I respond." I will keep this at the front of my mind and ask myself this question: What can I do in this moment? Sometimes there will be a lot I can do. Sometimes there won't. Perhaps all I can do is breathe, or say no, or walk away, or wait. No matter what the case is, there is always something that I can do. **I AM NEVER POWERLESS.**

Redirecting my energy and focus on whatever others are doing is not the answer either. I don't want to become a critic or judge of everyone else, attempting to control them as a way to divert from focusing on myself. What do *I* need to do to be better? How can *I* improve? Did *I* make the best choice? What do *I* need to change about me? That is where my focus should be. The only person I can control is me. This includes what I do, what I say, how I carry myself, how I spend my time and who I allow to enter my space. Those are all things that are in my control. That is where I will focus.

▲ Prayer ▲

Lord please help me to keep my focus on the right things; things that are within my control. Remind me that in every situation there is something I can do. Remind me that I am never powerless. Let me not get distracted by things that are not within my power to change. Help me not to focus on other people by trying to change them. That is your job Lord, not mine. I may have some influence, but my focus should still be on me.

Please forgive me for the times when I begin complaining and analyzing what another person could be doing. Your expectation of me is that I be responsible for myself and exercise my authority in all situations. Lord, I pray that you will give me a sense of direction of where to focus my energy. Let me not get stuck focusing on how something *should* have gone. Once it has already happened, all that can be decided is what to do next.

Lord, I know that the one thing I will always have is the power to choose. Let me stand firm in that power. In my power of choice lies my freedom. In the name of Jesus, I lift this prayer. ***Amen***.

▲ Action ▲

Check-in with yourself

Do I often get caught up in what other people should be doing? Do I overanalyze situations? Do I allow difficult situations to overwhelm me?

Make a choice

Today I choose to focus on what I can control because that's where my power is.

Act on your choice

≈ Always ask yourself, "What can I do about it right now?" and focus on that.

≈ Try not to rehearse the facts and get stuck in the emotion. It doesn't get you anywhere.

≈ Do not point the finger on what others can do. You can only control yourself.

CHAPTER TWELVE

Focus on Yourself and Not the World

"The Lord works from the inside out. The world works from the outside in. The world would take people out of the slums. Christ would take the slums out of people, and then they would take themselves out of the slums. The world would mold men by changing their environment. Christ changes men, who then change their environment. The world would shape human behavior, but Christ can change human nature."
—EZRA TAFT BENSON

"I have told you these things, so that in me you may have peace. In this world you will have trouble. But take heart! I have overcome the world."
—JOHN 16:33

▲ Affirmation ▲

I can't fix every problem in the world and God doesn't expect me to. The world is a complex place and it can be a cruel one too. There is a lot that goes on from day to day. Mass shootings, mass incarceration, modern day slavery, drug wars, sex trafficking, police shootings. There are all sorts of "isms" from racism to sexism to classism. It can be quite overwhelming. Although all these things are happening, my direct focus cannot be *everything* that is happening and I also can't allow it to be a major source for decision making in my personal life. Yes, there are ways for me to get involved and help but I can be aware and even be helpful without letting everything become my focus.

The truth is life will continue. The truth is the world is too large for me to solve all of its problems. The truth is there still is good happening in the world, even though it may not feel like it. There is no need for me to get overwhelmed by all the negative things that go on. I must find a way to show care and concern in a healthy way. If I focus just on the bad, it can paralyze me and disable me from doing the things that I need to do. I can refocus that energy towards doing what I can and leaving the rest to God.

▲ Prayer ▲

Lord at times all the evil in the world can feel like too much. Everywhere I turn there is something happening. I pray that you help me to not be overwhelmed by these things and trust that despite what it looks like, all things are working for my good.

God, I thank you that I have a heart to be concerned about these things and a heart that cares. Although I can begin to feel powerless over the many different situations that are happening around me, I trust that you will be pleased by my doing what I can to help. Remind me Lord that I cannot fix it all but in due time, you can, because you have overcome the world. I pray that you release me from creating a personal connection in an unhealthy way. Let me not internalize what is happening around me. Show me new ways to contribute to making this world a better place. Let me focus on what I can do and not on what I can't do.

Remind me that while there certainly are bad things happening, there is still much more good. Reassure me that I am protected despite it all and give me the faith that things will get better. In the name of Jesus, I life this prayer. *Amen.*

▲ Action ▲

Check-in with yourself

Am I often concerned about everything that is happening in the world? Do I feel powerless because of the many different types of issues that exist? Am I able to separate this from my day-to-day emotions and not get overwhelmed by it?

Make a choice

Today I choose to focus on myself and not the world because there is no way I can solve every problem.

Act on your choice

≈ Accept that it is impossible to tackle every problem in the world and God is not expecting you to do so.

≈ Do what you can to help. You cannot do everything but doing something counts. If a particular issue really impacts you, focus on a project to improve that issue or give a little to each cause.

CHAPTER THIRTEEN

Focus on Your Gifts

"Your talent is God's gift to you. What you do with it is your gift back to God."
—LEO BUSCAGLIA

"As each has received a gift, use it to serve one another, as good stewards of God's varied grace."
—1 PETER 4:10

▲ Affirmation ▲

There are people waiting on me to share my gifts. God placed me on this earth with many skills and talents so that I can share them with the world. Isn't that what gifts are for, to be given? This is not just about me, it's about who I can help and who I can touch just by simply being me and sharing what I have to give to this world. There are people who can benefit from my contribution no matter how small it may seem.

There may be others out there with similar abilities, but I don't have to be intimidated by that. I have something special that no one else has, that something is ME. When I bring together my essence and my spirit with my skills, gifts, and talents, I have something unique. No one can take it away from me because they didn't give it to me. I was born with it. The truth of the matter is, just like a snowflake, no two gifts are the same. They are each crystallized with their own unique imprint. No one has my vision or my mind.

It's not a competition. I don't have to be the next Beyoncé or the next Usain Bolt. I just have to be the best me and use my talents in the way that God called me to use them. I came here to do great works and that is what I will do. My gift does not have to be something entertaining or that reaches a million people. I may only reach a few. I need to be okay with that. When I use my gifts and others use their gifts, we create a win-win situation. I can connect with others on a deeper level through my talents and abilities. By using my gifts, I am deepening my connection with the world. I am growing and developing. The more I give and share, the more I create a space for new things to enter.

I realize that unless I put my gifts to use, I am doing myself and the world a huge disservice. I am essentially wasting time, not living life but letting it live me. There is no reason to keep my gifts all to myself. What would have happened if Dr. Martin Luther King, Jr. had not shared his gift of speaking and mobilizing masses? What would have happened if Steve Jobs hadn't shared his brilliant mind with the world and changed technology forever? I cannot stand by and waste what God has given me. I cannot be afraid to unleash the brilliance inside of me.

As I seek to share my gifts I will remember that God didn't place me here to have fame or possessions. Those things can be a byproduct of me using my gifts, but they are not the purpose. The truth is, those things may or may not come.

If God wants to use my gift to bless me financially, I won't turn it down. But I am not expecting that. I don't feel entitled to that. I am not sharing my gifts just for that. As long as I am just simply using and developing my gifts, I know that God will be pleased no matter what personal gains may come from it.

▲ Prayer ▲

Lord thank you for giving me so many skills, gifts, and talents. I pray that you help me to break through the fear of sharing all my gifts with the world. God, forgive me for the times when I have been selfish by keeping my gifts all to myself. That is not why you gave them to me. Lord you blessed me so that I can be a blessing to others. Let me not be worried about other people who may have similar talents and abilities. No matter what they have Lord, you made me unique in my own way.

What a shame it would be Lord, if I made it to the end of life to realize that I still had something left in me to share. I want to use every single thing that you've placed at my disposal. I want to share all that you've placed in my heart. Thank you for the many people who came before me and shared their gifts with the world. I am still benefiting from their contributions to this day. Remind me oh Lord, that it's not about fame or money. It's not about what I can gain but I can give. Help me to remember that I am sharing my gifts simply because that is what you called me to do. In the name of Jesus, I lift this prayer. **Amen**.

▲ Action ▲

Check-in with yourself

Am I using all the gifts God gave me? Are there things I could be sharing with the world that I am keeping to myself? Do I keep my gifts to myself because I feel there are too many other people doing what I want to do?

Make a choice

Today I choose to focus on my gifts because there are people in the world that are waiting on me to share them.

Act on your choice

≈ If you have many gifts, choose one to begin sharing now. Don't let the multiple interests overwhelm you. Be glad that you have more than one to choose from.

≈ Trust in your uniqueness. There may be other people doing what seems like the "same thing" but no one can do what you can do.

CHAPTER FOURTEEN

Focus on Solutions, Not Problems

"The truth is, you and I are in control of only two things: how we prepare for what might happen and how we respond to what just happened. The moment when things actually do happen belongs to God."
—DEVON FRANKLIN

"This is what the LORD says to you: 'Do not be afraid or discouraged because of this vast army. For the battle is not yours, but God's."
—2 CHRONICLES 20:15

▲ Affirmation ▲

My energy will either feed my faith or feed my fears. It can help me breakthrough or breakdown. It can make my problems better or worse. It's important for me to be clear that focusing on the negative is a choice and when I make a choice to be negative, that is the reality that I create for myself. Instead, I can choose to be solutions-focused. When difficult situations arise, I can ask myself, what can I do to fix this? How can I contribute to improving this situation? What resources do I have at my disposal that I can use as a catalyst for change? What can I do? I don't need to look outside of myself for the solution. I can't stand aside and wait for others to fix the problem. The answer is sometimes on the inside of me. There are pieces to a puzzle that only I possess. There is a way of thinking that only I possess. There is a swiftness of action that only I possess.

I. AM. THE. SOLUTION.

My mind is the solution. My ideas are the solution. My actions are the solution. The solution is inside of me.

Overanalyzing why something is happening or focusing on who is at fault or thinking of all the many things that can go wrong and all of the "what if" options, can waste valuable time. When I spend my time focused on the solution and not the problem I am being productive. I am expending my energy in the direction that I am seeking to go and not in the opposite direction. The problem has already happened. That means it is in the past. So, there is no need to get stuck there, looking behind. I can look forward and think about the outcome I want now, after the problem, and how to get there.

Being solutions-focused means I accept that there is always something that can be done. It doesn't mean that I will always get the best-case scenario. But it means that I understand there is always more to be gained from trying to find a solution than from staying focused on the problem. The truth is when I place a laser sharp focus on the issues at hand, I am giving them more power. They might already have some power but putting them under a microscope makes them that much worse. I may need to analyze and understand some facts needed to move forward, but not solely for the purpose of agonizing over the details.

Starting today, I am changing my attitude towards problems. It might take me some time to completely own this new disposition. There will be challenges that seem insurmountable and have real affects. But because I know the God I serve, I know that there will always be a solution. When issues arise, I will make a choice to use my energy to get beyond the problem. I am highly capable of problem solving. Optimism will become my way of life because I trust not only in my own capabilities but in the power of God.

▲ Prayer ▲

Lord thank you for gifting me with the ability to see beyond my present circumstances. In my daily life there are issues that arise, sometimes minor and sometimes major. Some of the problems I create on my own through how I think and where I focus my energy. Some of these issues, Lord, are REAL. They have real effects. But I know Lord that you will never give me something that I can't handle.

I know problems are a part of life. I've tackled many challenges; some I know for sure were only with your strength. But there are still times when I let issues get the best of me. I rehearse them over in my mind instead of getting to the solution. So, I am asking today Lord that you help me to grow in this area. God, I want to look at issues and challenges the way you do. I want to see a problem and say, "it's already fixed".

Help me to use my creativity and this brilliant mind you have given me to create new solutions. Let me not focus on what happened, why, and who's at fault when it isn't necessary or productive. Place my focus on what can be done and give me the swiftness of action to create a new reality beyond the problem. In the name of Jesus, I lift this prayer. *Amen*.

▲ Action ▲

Check-in with yourself

Do I often let my problems overtake me instead of focusing on a solution? Do difficult situations get the best of me? Do I sometimes feel helpless, like there is nothing I can do about a situation?

Make a choice

Today I choose to focus on solutions and not problems because there is always something I can do.

Act on your choice

≈ When you have a problem, step back and look at it from all angles to see what the best approach is.

≈ Talk to someone who is good at problem solving. They may have an idea that you can't see.

≈ Refrain from rehearsing what can't be done. There is no power there.

PART IV

• • •

What to Learn

CHAPTER FIFTEEN

Learn to Say No

"To do big things, you have to say "no" to a lot of average things."
—UNKNOWN

"But let your 'Yes' be 'Yes,' and your 'No,' 'No.'"
—MATTHEW 5:37

▲ Affirmation ▲

I have choices in life and I have a right to express those choices. I will not be a "Yes man" or "Yes woman", just saying yes to everything that comes my way. Instead, I will make a decision about what is worth my "Yes" and what is not. When I say "Yes" to everything without consideration to how it can impact me and my purpose, I am operating on autopilot. That is not how I want to be. I know there is power in my choice and I commit to using it.

There is just as much power in my "No" as there is in my "Yes". When I say "No" to the things that don't serve me, I am saying "Yes" to the things that do serve me. It's not about other people and what they want or need from me, it is about me. I have an obligation to myself to ensure that my commitments are aligned with my spirit and the vision that I have for myself now and in the future. Whether or not people understand, is not my worry. They are responsible for their choices and I am responsible for mine.

Saying "No" does not make me mean or inconsiderate; it simply means I am making a choice for me. I have no intention of hurting other people or becoming self-centered. While I always want to be sure that I am making a sound choice and being considerate of others, I also want to be sure not to overextend myself at the detriment of my own well-being. As long as I express myself with love and care, I can feel confident that my integrity is in check.

There will be times when I need to support my friends or do things for my family even when I don't feel like it. Those are things I actually want to do. So, I will not use the power of my "No" as a means to neglect prioritizing things that should be important to me. It all comes back to what I place value in. Once I have a clear set of values and boundaries, the things I say "Yes" to and the things I say "No" to become easier to differentiate.

The power of my choice also helps me to take responsibility for the things in my life. What am I saying "Yes" to and how is that affecting me? What am I am saying "No" to and how is that affecting me? These are things I will consider as I seek to make sure that I am making the best choices for my life.

▲ Prayer ▲

Lord, please help me to decide the things that are worthy of my "Yes" and the things that are not. Let me not be afraid to say "No" to the things that don't honor my spirit. There are things that are simply not aligned with what you have for me. Help me to turn away from things easily.

Remove from me the need to justify my "No" and let me not feel guilty for saying it. Let me be able to say "No" to the people or things that threaten my peace with ease. God, I want to be honorable in my decisions and consider how I impact others, but I don't want to be a pushover. I don't want people to come to expect from me a "Yes", every time they ask because it is not realistic. So, God, let me stand firm on my word knowing that it comes from a place of goodness.

Lord, please help me to take responsibility for the choices in my life. You have given me power and free will. I trust that you have already revealed in my spirit the things that are good for me. Please help me to honor those things not just for who I am now, but also for who I hope to be. In the name of Jesus, I lift this prayer. ***Amen***.

▲ Action ▲

Check-in with yourself

Do I just say "Yes" to everything without thinking of my commitment? Am I afraid to say "No" to the things and people that don't serve me? Has saying "Yes" to things I don't want caused me to get the short end of the stick?

Make a choice

Today I choose to say "No" to what I <u>don't</u> want because then I can say "Yes" to what I <u>do</u> want.

Act on your choice

≈ Prioritize. Know where your values lie so you can decide what to say "Yes" to and what to say "No" to.

≈ Stop feeling bad about it. If you cannot attend an event or lend someone money (for the one hundredth time), say no. And don't feel guilty about it.

≈ Be Polite. Saying "No" should not come off as mean, arrogant, or selfish. It's all about how you say it and the context of the situation.

CHAPTER SIXTEEN

Learn to Put Yourself First

"When you take time to replenish your spirit, it allows you to serve others from the overflow. You cannot serve from an empty vessel."
—ELEANOR BROWN

"What you are doing is not good. You and these people who come to you will only wear yourselves out."
—EXODUS 18:17

▲ Affirmation ▲

My first responsibility is to myself. If I don't take care of myself, there is no way that I can be good to others. I will take the time I need to keep myself mentally, physically, emotionally, and spiritually filled so that I can be my best. I cannot be my best if I am always drained and not at full capacity. When my mind, body, and spirit are fully functioning because they have been nourished, that is when I can thrive.

I cannot put everyone else before me. Yes, I love my friends and family, but I love myself more. How well I take care of myself sets the standard for everyone around me. If I am not treating myself well, how can I expect others to treat me well? It starts with me. Even if I am in a relationship, I still need to take time for myself. There is a special type of care and love that comes from self that no one else can give.

So, no matter how busy it gets, I will find a moment to take care of me. I will prioritize time to spoil myself and treat myself like royalty. I cannot put everyone else first and go above and beyond for others at the expense of my own well-being. I come first! I matter most!

▲ Prayer ▲

Lord, please show me how to put myself first. I take great pride in caring for those who I love. Sometimes Lord my good heart causes me to put others before myself. There are even times when I forget about myself altogether. I know there are times when I must make sacrifices and I don't intend to be self-centered. But help me to see that I can only be good to those I love if I am good to myself first. Don't allow me to do more for others than I do for myself. Let me be number one in my life always.

Remind me oh Lord that it is me who sets the standard for others on how I should be treated. Let the level of concern and care that I have for myself be an example for those around me. God, I don't want to depend on other people to take care of me. What others do for me cannot replace the things I do for myself.

I pray Lord that you will place in my spirit a sense of urgency around taking care of me. When things get busy, help me to find the time to ensure that I am well. Remind me that if I am not well, nothing else matters. In the name of Jesus, I lift this prayer. *Amen.*

▲ Action ▲

Check-in with yourself

Am I always going above and beyond for everyone else and not for me? How often do I take time for myself? When was the last time I took myself out or treated myself?

Make a choice

Today I choose to put myself first because I am the most important person in my life.

Act on your choice

≈ *Take yourself on a date!* You can go to the movies, dinner, a comedy show, a museum. Whatever you choose, spending quality time alone is one of the best gifts you will ever give yourself.

≈ *Treat yourself to a massage!* Find a masseuse you like and set up a regularly scheduled appointment. Your body will thank you for it.

≈ *Go to the doctor!* Knowing you're healthy is the most important thing you can do to show your love for yourself. Your health is the foundation for everything else you do.

CHAPTER SEVENTEEN

Learn to Live in the Now

"Living in the moment means letting go of the past and not waiting for the future. It means living your life consciously, aware that each moment you breathe is a gift."
–OPRAH WINFREY

"Therefore, do not worry about tomorrow, for tomorrow will worry about itself. Each day has enough trouble of its own."
—MATTHEW 6:34

▲ Affirmation ▲

The best times are not behind me or in front of me. The best time is right now. Honestly, now is all I have. I am not promised tomorrow and yesterday is gone. I will get all that I can out of this present moment. When I think about it, most of my frustration comes from either living in the past and wishing it was different, or living in the future where I think things will be so much better. But what I have in my future is partly a result of what I do now. There are seeds that I can sow now so they can be ready when the harvest comes. There are things I can be doing right now. I'm not going to live my life always in the "when I" season. *When I* make enough money, *when I* get my house, *when I* meet my spouse. I can decide that I will be whatever it is that I am seeking to be right here and now. If I want to be happy I will do so now with whatever I have. I don't have to live in the future. I can live in the now.

I will challenge myself to be present in every moment. When my mind starts to drift to what I did already or what I need to do, I will bring it back to the present moment. The truth of the matter is, there are many things I can't do anything about right now. But there is always something I *can* do. I will ask myself, what can I be doing about it now? Is this something I need to focus on now? I can suck the joy out of a moment by not being present, overanalyzing, or thinking of things that will probably never happen. Instead, I will try not to think too deeply into things and learn to just simply enjoy the moment. This way I can be happier, calmer, and more appreciative.

▲ Prayer ▲

Lord, let me be able to enjoy the moments I experience, not taking them for granted. Tomorrow is not promised, so I want to appreciate what you have for me now. I know that the present moment is where my power and joy live. Help me to stay focused on the now.

Give me the peace of knowing that everything I have experienced up until this point was meant to be a part of my story, so there is no need to rehearse the past. Being in the past and future will only give me frustration. I don't want to be frustrated Lord. I want to be at peace. Remind me that nothing that you have for me has or will miss me. Help me to let go of any guilt or anger from the past that is impacting my ability to enjoy the present.

While the future is certainly something to look forward to, help me not put off things that I can be doing now. Show me how to sow seeds now that will reap benefits later. Let me take advantage of everything that I can be doing in this season to prepare me for when the harvest comes. In the name of Jesus, I lift this prayer. *Amen*.

▲ Action ▲

Check-in with yourself

Do I often think about the past or the future? Do I have a hard time focusing on the present moment?

Make a choice

Today I choose to live in the now because it's all that I am guaranteed.

Act on your choice

≈ Try to enjoy a day out without taking excessive photos. The memories are important, but you definitely miss out on things if you're only snapping away.

≈ Leave your phone in the car or put it away when you're out with other people. If you went out with them it's to enjoy their company. Instagram and Facebook will still be there when you are done. Enjoy the presence of your company!

≈ Try to take notice of what's happening in the moment. Just enjoy what's around as you go about each day.

CHAPTER EIGHTEEN

Learn to Embrace Challenges

"Challenges are gifts that force us to search for a new center of gravity. Don't fight them. Just find a new way to stand."
—OPRAH WINFREY

"Consider it pure joy, my brothers and sisters, whenever you face trials of many kinds, because you know that the testing of your faith produces perseverance. Let perseverance finish its work so that you may be mature and complete, not lacking anything. "
—JAMES 1:2-4

▲ Affirmation ▲

Difficult times are inevitable especially when I am chasing my purpose. Because I have big dreams and goals, it's unrealistic that I will not experience struggle. It comes with the territory of greatness. Trying to reach my goals will not be an easy feat. If it were easy, it probably wouldn't be worth it. There will be moments on my journey when I get stressed, frustrated, fed up, hopeless, scared, and tired.

The. Struggle. Is. Real.

But God already gave me all the tools I need to survive these moments. It's important that I remember that it's simply a part of the journey. It's not meant to break me down but to build me up. So, when the tough times come I will remember that it is all part of the plan. Instead of allowing them to throw me off course, I will use them as building blocks as I press forward toward the mark.

God already knew that there would be challenges, so he gave me the tools necessary to withstand them. In fact, he created many circumstances specifically to grow and strengthen me. He did this to bring out of me the creativity and courage that I didn't know was deep within. I don't have to be afraid just because something looks hard. I don't have to back down just because of a setback. I don't have to throw in the towel because someone said "No" once, twice, or even twenty times. These difficulties are a part of the journey.

The challenge will respond to whatever disposition I have. If I approach it with anticipation, it loses its power. If I approach it looking for an opportunity within it, it loses its power. If my vision is greater than the challenge, it loses its power. Difficulty doesn't have to make me desperate. I can stand firm even in the face of hardships if I remember who I am and who God is. I've already proven that I can handle tough things. This isn't my first rodeo. Some of the things I've tackled should've killed me, BUT GOD! God's power makes mountains look like anthills, makes crossing oceans feel like jumping puddles, makes an enemy into a foot stool. God specializes in difficulty, so I have nothing to be afraid of. I will not run, back down or give up. No. I will embrace the challenges knowing that there is nothing but greatness to be gained.

▲ Prayer ▲

Lord I thank you for giving me challenges that grow and strengthen me. Although it doesn't feel good in the moment, I know that difficulties are just meant to show me what I'm made of. Don't let me grow weary when the challenges come. Give me a strong mind to know that it's all a part of the process. When I get wrapped up in my expectancy that now should be better than it is, remind me that I am working towards something greater. Let the difficulties be a sign that I am headed in the right direction. Everything will not be roses and sunflowers. This I know Lord. But you built me for this. Let me remember that all that I'm working for will reap its benefits in due time.

Give me the strength and tenacity Lord to push ahead when the storms come. Help me to understand that it has to rain down water, in order for my seeds to grow. Growth can't come from dry ground. There will need to be some storms Lord. Father I know that you've given me all I need to survive every attack of the enemy. You know every plot and plan. You've already made a way for me. I don't need to stress myself out trying to figure out why I'm having a certain experience or when it will pass, because I trust that you wouldn't steer me wrong Lord. You're always working on my behalf. Even if things don't seem like they will work out, you always make sure they do. So, I will not worry. I will trust and fight on. In the name of Jesus, I lift this prayer. *Amen*.

▲ Action ▲

Check-in with yourself

Do I get caught off guard by challenges? Am I meeting challenges with the expectation that they will be resolved? Does difficulty make me back down?

Make a choice

Today I choose to embrace challenges because that is the only way I can grow.

Act on your choice

≈ When challenges come, don't panic. Meet them with expectancy and remind yourself it's already done. There is no need to worry.

≈ Think about how you can grow and stretch yourself. Every challenge gives you something to learn. Most importantly you get to see what you're really made of.

CHAPTER NINETEEN

Learn to Set Boundaries

"Walls keep everybody out boundaries teach people where the door is."
—MARK GROVES

"Even as I try to please everyone in every way. For I am not seeking my own good but the good of many, so that they may be saved."
—1 CORINTHIANS 10:33

▲ Affirmation ▲

The open-door policy approach does not apply to my life. People cannot just walk in and do whatever they want to do. I set clear boundaries so that the people in my life know how I expect to be treated, what's important to me, and what I will and won't allow. This isn't a matter of being too strict or inflexible, but it ensures that I have some level of peace. If I don't establish boundaries, then I can't be surprised when people mistreat me, use me, or are inconsiderate. There are dreams and plans connected to me. I need to be protective of those dreams and plans. I cannot allow anything or anyone to derail the vision that God has for my life by not having boundaries.

When people are around me they will know that honesty is expected, respect is expected, and consideration is expected. In my circle, we don't put others down. We don't thrive off dysfunction and drama. We don't do things that are displeasing to God. We can be mature, serve God, and still have fun. There is nothing unattractive about being positive. It's all about balance. Those are the kinds of boundaries I need. Through my actions I demonstrate to others what I will and won't allow. If need be, I will express my expectations through conversation but not much has to be said when my actions show others who I am and what I'm about.

I won't allow people to use me two, three, and four times. The people in my life don't get to borrow money from me and not pay it back unless that is what we've agreed to. The people in my life don't get to speak to me in a disrespectful manner. The people in my life don't get to withdraw and never deposit. I draw the line as a sign of respect to myself. There are limits that have to be set in my life. When my boundaries are not respected, it's important that I communicate what my limits are. I cannot expect that people will just automatically know and respect them. And then I must be prepared to make a decision if those limits are pushed, which can mean altering or ending the relationship if necessary. I cannot afford to be drained, frustrated, and hurt because of other people's lack of concern for my needs. Since I know that I will reciprocate, it is within my best interest to have these boundaries in place.

▲ Prayer ▲

Lord, my kindhearted nature is an absolute blessing. I am grateful for a heart like yours. You've shown me how to be accepting, open, and giving to others. I thank you for that. But God, I am asking that you help me to know how to create healthy boundaries. I am not trying to cut people off or create a presence where people don't feel free to be themselves. I truly want to have the best of times with those I love and care about. However, I know that the things you are asking of me will require me to be clear about what is allowed in my space. Everything matters when I am chasing your will Lord. There are things I know you have for me and I cannot achieve those things if I allow the people around me to do things that are counter to your vision.

God, how I allow people to treat me and treat others says a lot about me. I know you didn't create me in your divine image to be walked over Lord. You are expecting me to be intentional on this journey and set an example. So, God I pray for discernment on where to draw the line. I have faith that with your guidance I can maintain healthy relationships that honor me and honor your plans for my life. In the name of Jesus, I lift this prayer. **Amen**.

▲ Action ▲

Check-in with yourself

Are people allowed to do whatever they want in my life? Do I end up getting used? Do people take advantage of me? Do I struggle with setting boundaries and sticking to them?

Make a choice

Today I choose to set boundaries because I need to protect my space.

Act on your choice

≈ Don't be afraid to put people on the 'blocked list' in order to preserve your peace.

≈ Speak up and let people know what works for you and what doesn't.

≈ Be willing to let go of people who don't seem to respect your space.

CHAPTER TWENTY

Learn to Wait

"The wait is a two-way street. God does some of the work, but you have to do your share."
— DEVON FRANKLIN

"I wait for the LORD, my soul waits, And in His word, I do hope."
—PSALM 130:5

▲ Affirmation ▲

Not everything can happen for me overnight. Most great things don't. I can make the choice to either get the microwaved version of what I want or to wait for the real deal. When I rush to get something, there is a lot that is missed. Deeper experiences, opportunities, and lessons might pass me by because I'm in a rush. God may want to speak to me and guide me through the process to get an even better outcome than I expected, but if I'm too busy rushing and just trying get instant gratification, I may miss those things. I have to remind myself that whatever is meant for me will not miss me. I don't have to fear that if I don't rush to get it or have it now, then it may not be mine. God doesn't work like that. He is not here to trick me out of the things he has for me.

Waiting is not just a choice, it is a skill. Although it is not easy to do, once I master the art of waiting, I unlock a greater potential for myself. Some of the things I'm hoping for will require me to wait, to have patience. Sometimes I just need to slow down and wait on a word from God. I don't have the green light to proceed sometimes. It's important that I wait. If I ask God for a sign and I feel like he doesn't respond right away, that doesn't mean I can assume I should just go ahead. That may not be the case. He might need to work some details out first or move some things around. I have to learn how to be patient while the Lord does his work, trusting that all of it will work in my favor.

I have to maintain a delicate balance while waiting in order for it to be effective. I cannot just sit around and do absolutely nothing and claim that I am waiting on God. No, no, no. That is not how this works. I can't use waiting as an excuse or as a mechanism to get away with not doing what I'm supposed to do. Waiting means that I wait for what God promises me instead of taking a counterfeit. That means I wait on a relationship that serves me, instead of jumping into a relationship with just anyone. That means I wait for a job offer that pays me my worth instead of taking just any job. In order for the wait to work I have to be clear on what God told me he had for me to begin with. This way, when something comes along that doesn't fit God's promise, I can peacefully say: I'll wait.

▲ Prayer ▲

Lord, teach me how to wait in peace. It's not easy but help me to not rush or be tempted by the other things that come along. Don't let me be fooled by the other things that come to stand in the way of your promise just because I simply cannot wait. I've learned that everything that glitters isn't gold. And I've also learned that the devil specializes in glitter making. I do not want the false promises Lord, I want what you *really* have for me.

I ask you to build up in me the tenacity to wait. I know that in the waiting I will gain many things that I will need in order to maintain the promises you've given to me. It's not just about getting the promise, Lord but maintaining it. Give me strength and courage to see your promises through until the end. I know that there is greater to be gained when I wait it out.

While I wait show me what it is that I need to see. I know there are experiences and opportunities that are connected to my waiting. Lord, help me to discern when to wait and when to move. Keep my spiritual intuition clear so that I will know what to do. In the name of Jesus, I lift this prayer. ***Amen.***

▲ Action ▲

Check-in with yourself

Do I often rush into things? Do I have a hard time waiting? Has my inability to wait caused me to get less than what I deserved in the past?

Make a choice

Today I choose to wait because by waiting I get access to the *best* of what God has for me.

Act on your choice

≈ Wait for the green light from God before proceeding. Rushing into something without God's approval is a recipe for disaster.

≈ Cut off things that make it hard for you to wait. If something or someone is tempting you to give in, remove them.

≈ Discern counterfeits that come to take the place of God's promise. You will know if it's what he really has for you.

≈ Enjoy the wait. You don't have to wait in misery. Focus on how blessed you'll be because of it.

PART V

...

What to Be

CHAPTER TWENTY-ONE

Be Grateful

"Gratitude unlocks the fullness of life. It turns what we have into enough, and more. It turns denial into acceptance, chaos to order, confusion to clarity. It can turn a meal into a feast, a house into a home, a stranger into a friend."
—MELODY BEATTIE

"Therefore, let us be grateful for receiving a kingdom that cannot be shaken, and thus let us offer to God acceptable worship, with reverence and awe."
—HEBREWS 12:28

▲ Affirmation ▲

I have so much to be grateful for. There is no second of the day that I'm not blessed. The moment I open my eyes, I am blessed. Just waking up is a blessing. I am grateful for the air in my lungs, for having another day to live, and for the opportunity to pursue a fulfilling life. I am grateful for God's endless provision, protection, and presence. In this moment, I am reminded that all my needs are met. There is nothing I am lacking. God has provided it all. There are many things seen and unseen that God protects me from. And with all the violence and negativity that happens every day, I know for sure that I am a walking miracle. I am protected everywhere I go. I am grateful that God sees fit to keep me here. As I move through life, I do not walk alone. God's presence is always with me. He walks with me, talks with me, and lets me know that I am his. God is always guiding and directing my steps. He shows me when to stop and be cautious and when to proceed ahead.

As I move throughout the day, I will be more aware of all there is to appreciate around me, big things and small things alike. I will not take for granted the things that God blesses me with daily. It is through my gratitude that I show

God I am ready for more. Being grateful for what I have, opens the door for what I want. If I can't appreciate what's in front of me NOW, how can God trust that I will appreciate the greater things he has in store for me?

I'm grateful for all the lessons I learned through the hard times and all the times I thought I couldn't make it through, but I did. What has not killed me, has made me stronger. I know that things could always be worse. Things *have* been worse. But my good days *always* outweigh my bad days. I won't complain. There is someone out there experiencing a true life or death situation, so I dare not be ungrateful! Whether or not things go as planned, if I don't get what I wanted from a situation, if the trials and tribulations come — **I'll. Still. Be. Grateful.**

I will not wait until it's too late to show the people in my life that I appreciate them. I may not have another day. So, today is the day. The people I love and care for will know it through the words I speak to them and things I do for them while they are still here. They deserve to know how important they are. They deserve to know that they are loved.

▲ Prayer ▲

Lord thank you for the countless things you bless me with daily. Even if you never bless me with another thing, you have already done enough. You don't have to *show out,* for me to be appreciative. Teach me to be more aware of every blessing, big or small.

Although I may go through "bad" times, help me to be grateful for all experiences. Your word says that all things work together for the good of those who love you. Thank you for making even the bad things work in my favor. Show me how to see the good in every situation for I know you make no mistakes.

God, I thank you for the people you have placed in my life. Please help me to appreciate them while they are still here. Let them feel loved by my words and my actions. Bless and keep them Lord.

Forgive me for times when I do not appreciate things as much as I should. And if you catch me being ungrateful Lord, straighten me out. Remind me what I've been through and what others are going through. Keep my gratitude cup filled at all times. In the name of Jesus, I lift this prayer. *Amen.*

▲ Action ▲

Check-in with yourself

Do I take time to be grateful daily? When was the last time I sent someone a tangible thank you gift?

Make a choice

Today I choose to be grateful because I am blessed beyond measure.

Act on your choice

≈ Make a note of the things you are grateful for daily. It can be a mental note, a gratitude journal, or you can write them down on index cards and place the cards in a jar.

≈ Say thank you. Think of the last person who did something nice for you or made you smile. Send that person a gift, a thank you note, a thank you text, or buy a card as a gesture of your thanks.

≈ Pay more attention to the "little" things. As you go throughout the day, try to find new things to be grateful for, things you would not ordinarily be aware of.

CHAPTER TWENTY-TWO

Be Clear About What You Want Out of Life

"When you have clarity of intention, the universe conspires with you to make it happen."
—FABIENNE FREDERICKSON

"And those he predestined, he also called; those he called, he also justified; those he justified, he also glorified."
—ROMANS 8:30

▲ Affirmation ▲

Anything I want can be mine by the grace of God. The desires of my heart are connected to my purpose. It is my responsibility to nurture those desires and manifest the destiny God has created for me. God would not give me a vision and a hope that he cannot fulfill. He has already equipped me with every tool, every thought, every idea, and every ounce of strength needed to fulfill his vision for my life.

Having clarity about what I want allows the universe to shift in my favor. By declaring my vision, I will attract into my life the people and resources that I need to see it come to pass. Every area of my life is connected to this vision: my finances, my health, my family and friends, and my career and life purpose. When the vision is clear, all these things begin to align. It gives my life intention and purpose.

My dreams matter. My purpose matters, I matter. I have everything I need to go after what I want. I don't want to leave this world without having tried my best to pursue my desires. I would rather die trying.

▲ Prayer ▲

Lord, I thank you for the desires of my heart. Not only do you know exactly what I need, but you also know my wants. God, I am yearning for the fullness of the life you have for me. My soul desires more. I know that you created me for great things. Help me to be clear about my purpose and your vision for my life.

I thank you in advance for the people and resources you will place into my life. Send me purpose mates God, people who can help me achieve the vision you have for me. I pray that I not only will be blessed by them but that I may also be a blessing to them in the process.

God, there is not a single thing you have for me that I want to leave on the table. No stone unturned. I want it all Lord. Let not a single thing go to waste. Show me how to use the tools you have given me to fulfill my life's purpose. If I begin to doubt my abilities or my worthiness please remind me that you have equipped me with everything that I need. You would not give me desires that you know cannot be fulfilled. In the name of Jesus, I lift this prayer. *Amen.*

▲ Action ▲

Check-in with yourself

Am I clear about what I want out of life? Do I have goals? Do I have a short-term and long-term vision?

Make a choice

Today I choose to get clear about what I want out of life because without a vision I cannot begin to manifest my dreams.

Act on your choice

≈ Create a vision board. By mapping out images that represent your hopes and dreams, you create a clear point of reference by which you can align your actions. You can download images and then use a collage app (such as LiveCollage) to group them together instead of cutting out pictures from magazines.

≈ Recite daily affirmations. When you recite affirmations, you are declaring to the universe that your desire will be met. You can start by turning your desires into "I am", "I will" or "I have" statements. Ex: I am a best-selling author.

CHAPTER TWENTY-THREE

Be Intentional With Your Time

"Change your 24 hours and you will change your life."
—ERIC THOMAS

"Teach us to number our days, that we may gain a heart of wisdom."
—PSALM 90:12

▲ Affirmation ▲

My time is precious. I only have so much of it this lifetime. Once it is gone, I cannot get it back. The way I spend it tells God a lot about whether or not I view it as a gift. It is up to me to spend my time in a way that best serves and on things that will ground me and grow me in order to help me get the most out of life, The vision that I have for my life can only come to pass if I am actively working towards it using the time that I have. I will need to think through what I'm doing on a daily basis, and make decisions about things that I want to spend more time on and less time on. God gave me the purpose, but he cannot force me to spend the time necessary to follow it.

I have to be mindful not to confuse busy with productive and take a step back to see if what I am doing is actually producing results. Sometimes there will be slow traction as I am trying to build my vision. However, spending a lot of time on things that just don't work will not help me in the long run. With a clear intention and focus I can make the best use of the time I have instead of letting things just happen.

Prioritizing the things that are fulfilling is the best way to ensure my time is spent wisely. While social media, television, and games might help me to relax, wasting countless hours of time on them is not only unproductive but can detract from my mental state. These things might be fun, but they will not help me to get to where I am trying to go.

Planning how I'm going to spend my day is an important practice in using the time that I have to manifest the things I want. If I am not spending time on bettering myself, then how can I expect my dreams to come true? My priorities don't just fall into place. Scheduling time to make things happen is the only way they will.

There are many things that God can do, but he can only do them if I am moving and actively doing the things I need to do. If I am stagnant and idle, the Holy Spirit cannot do its best work in me. Idleness is the devils playground. When I don't make good use of my time, it gets filled with things I don't want, don't need, or that simply don't serve me.

I don't have to have everything figured out in order to make a move. Whether or not I am fully clear, I will move forward and learn along the way. As I begin to move, I learn what works and what doesn't, what sits well with my spirit and what doesn't, what I like and what I don't like. I am not moving blindly if I know what my purpose is. The key is to make use of the time I have.

▲ Prayer ▲

Lord, thank you for the gift of time. I will not take this time for granted because I know that it is not promised. Each moment that you give me is another chance to be my best. I appreciate the time I am able to spend with family and friends, enjoy the simple things in life, and create a better life for myself and those around me. Help me to not take this time for granted. I want to make use of every moment to the best of my ability.

Please help me to spend my time wisely. Let me not be distracted by being busy instead of being productive. I want to actually produce results and move towards the vision you have for my life, Lord. Help me to not spend an unhealthy amount of time on social media or television. If there are people or things that are not worth my time, block them out Lord. Let me be decisive about my time. Remind me that I don't have much of it.

God, I know you can only do your best work if I am doing my part. So, I pray that you will push me through any moments of stagnation. When I feel stuck, please remove whatever it is that is blocking me from moving forward. In the name of Jesus, I lift this prayer. *Amen.*

▲ Action ▲

Check-in with yourself

Do I waste a lot of time on entertainment like social media and TV, daily? Am I scheduling time for what's important to me? Is most of my time productive or unproductive?

Make a choice

Today I choose to be intentional with my time because I only have so much of it.

Act on your choice

≈ Create a schedule. Having a schedule will help you to stay on track with the priorities in your life. Schedule the time for the things that are important in your life!

≈ Cutback on time wasters. There is nothing wrong with a little television, social media, or games. Indulge a bit but be careful not to go overboard. The worst thing you can do is come to the realization that the time you could have spent on your dreams was wasted carelessly.

CHAPTER TWENTY-FOUR

Be Kind and Loving

"I know of only one duty, and that is to love."
—ALBERT CAMUS

"Above all, love each other deeply, because love covers over a multitude of sins."
—1 PETER 4:8

▲ Affirmation ▲

How I treat others says a lot about who I am. I will treat others with love and kindness because that's what I want to receive. I cannot expect that people will give me what I am not giving to them. In my daily interactions, I will seek to spread joy, love, and happiness no matter what is happening around me. This is not about other people, this is about me and God. God has called me to be loving to my fellow brothers and sisters. That is what I will do.

We are all navigating this life in the best way we know how. We don't always show the best of ourselves. I may encounter people who aren't showing the best of themselves, but they are still worthy of my love and kindness. As I move throughout the day I will cut a little slack to those around me. If someone doesn't say excuse me, it's still love. If someone isn't being mindful of others, it's still love. It's not about what they are doing. It's about me and what I am doing. It's absolutely about what God expects of me.

There may be people suffering around me, sometimes in silence. I will seek to spread a little love to that person. Just a smile will do. Just an extra minute or two to hold the door for someone will do. Just a "Good Morning" will do.

Just a "How are you today?" will do. An "I love you" will do. An "I appreciate you" will do. An "I apologize" will do.

When there are disagreements, I will approach them from a place of love. Everything does not have to be a knockout, drag out argument. If this is a person I love, I will talk to them as such, no matter what their stance may be. I will ask myself "What would love do?" The people I love will know it by what I say to them, how I speak to them, how I treat them. Love will be in every word, in every touch and in every effort that I make.

There is already enough hatred. There is more than enough evil. There is a ton of bad intentions. I will not contribute to this already stirring pot. Instead I will stir in the opposite direction. Just a drop of my love and kindness can overpower ten times the amount of hate and evil in the world. I will continue loving and giving until it spreads like wildfire to every person around me, inspires them to do the same, and changes the world even if just a bit.

▲ Prayer ▲

Lord thank you for giving me a big heart. Thank you for gifting me with a spirit of love and kindness. Help me to use this love I have in ways unimaginable. Help me to use this love I have to create new possibilities. Let me not be afraid to share my love with those around me, because we all need it. God as I move throughout my day let me be attentive to the people around me who need a little love and kindness. Let me not be so selfish and wrapped up in myself that I forget the people around me who need my love, need my smile, need my caring, need my concern and need my kindness.

Lord, there may have been times when people didn't appreciate me and all I had to give. But don't let that harden me to love. Remind me oh God, that it's not about them but it's about you. It's about what you asked me to be. It's about who you made me to be. Keep my mind on this in those times when people make it difficult to love. It's never difficult when it's for you Lord. I do it all for your Glory. I know that there is much more to be gained from loving and giving than there is from keeping it all to myself. Pull the love out of me if you have to Lord, and use it for your purpose. In the name of Jesus, I lift this prayer. *Amen.*

▲ Action ▲

Check-in with yourself

Do I treat people with kindness and love; even strangers? Am I expecting love and kindness, yet I am not giving it? Does my love and kindness get thrown out the window when I'm mad?

Make a choice

Today I choose to be kind and loving because that is what God expects of me and that is what I want to receive.

Act on your choice

≈ Perform random acts of kindness such as buying a meal for a homeless person.

≈ Smile and say good morning to the people you come into contact with.

≈ Do something special for a friend or family member.

≈ Hold the door for the person behind you.

CHAPTER TWENTY-FIVE

Be Faithful

"Faith is taking the first step even when you don't see the whole staircase. "
—MARTIN LUTHER KING, JR.

"So that your faith might not rest on human wisdom, but on God's power."
—1 CORINTHIANS 2:5

▲ Affirmation ▲

I believe deep in the core of my soul that God has plans to prosper me and not to harm me. If his word says it, then it is true. There is no need for me to doubt or worry about what will happen. I may not know how or when it is going to happen, but I do know for sure that all things will work out for my good. God has already proven himself time and time again. His faithfulness has been shown to me in big ways, little ways, subtle ways, direct ways, expected ways, unexpected ways, deserving ways, undeserving ways, when I needed it, when I didn't, when I wanted it and when I didn't.

God. Has. Been. There.

God has been there for me more than my friends could ever be. They love me. It's no offense to them, but when it comes to being there, God has them beat. The same is true for my family or anyone else. Again, I appreciate what they've done for me, but they haven't done what God has done. No one can do what God can do. No one.

My relationship with God is built on trust and a deep belief that his protection, provision, and presence will always be with me. With this in mind, I will step out on faith believing that God will cover me all the way through. He will not ask me to take a leap without equipping me for the landing. He would not tell me to go for something without knowing that I have all I need to bring the victory home. He created me with everything I need to accomplish the purpose he has for me. I don't need to search anywhere for it. It is already within me. That is why I can have faith.

When doubt starts to creep into my mind, I will remember who God is and what he has already done. I will remember that I am not just talking about any ol' body. I am talking about God. The Alpha and Omega. The Most High. The One who formed me in my mother's womb with purpose and intent. I'm not going to insult God by not having Faith. My faith shows God that I really know him and believe in his power. It shows God that I trust in him and his abilities. It shows God that I appreciate what he has already done. I will stand on my faith today, tomorrow, and always. In good times and bad, on my faith I will stand.

▲ Prayer ▲

Lord thank you for always being there for me. Even when I felt like I didn't deserve your love, you were there showing me grace and mercy. You've given me chance after chance. God you make believing so easy. You show me new wonders each day to remind me of how powerful you are, and yet it still can be hard to have faith all the time. But I thank you for continuing to strengthen my faith each day. I'm thankful that even a mustard seed of faith is enough for you to work with.

When my faith starts to falter, Lord, remind me of the time when you saved Daniel from the Lion's Den. Remind me of the time you saved Shadrach, Meshach, and Abednego from the fiery furnace. Remind me of the time you saved Jonah from the belly of the fish. If you did it for them, I know you will do it for me. It may not always look like things will work out in my favor Lord. In those times remind me of who you are and what you do best. In faith, your power is magnified. When I combine my faith with your power, it's a match made in heaven. Things begin to move, walls begin to fall, enemies begin to fold. Faith is the cure for many things.

Father, you are my light and salvation, whom shall I fear? Whom shall I be afraid? Help me to believe in you Lord so that I can believe in me. Help me to have faith in my own power. Without you I may not be able to do it, but I have to remember Lord that I am not working alone. You are with me. The Holy Spirit is dwelling within me. Please keep strengthening my faith Lord. In the name of Jesus, I lift this prayer. *Amen.*

▲ Action ▲

Check-in with yourself

Do I often doubt God in tough situations? Have I taken any leaps of faith in my life trusting that God would see me through? Do I need to see in order to believe or can I just trust God?

Make a choice

Today I choose to be faithful because I know that God will never fail me.

Act on your choice

≈ When you're in a tough situation, remember that God has never failed you and he will not start now.

≈ Take a leap of faith on something that's big and trust that God will see you through it.

CHAPTER TWENTY-SIX

Be Reflective

"Self-awareness is our capacity to stand apart from ourselves and examine our thinking, our motives, our history, our scripts, our actions, and our habits and tendencies."
—STEPHEN COVEY

"Let us examine our ways and test them, and let us return to the Lord."
—LAMENTATIONS 3:40

▲ Affirmation ▲

I cannot go through each day just letting things happen to me. With all the many things that go on throughout the day, week, month, and year, it's important that I take a step back to understand and assess what is happening around me and ask myself some key questions. How am I feeling? Is there anything that isn't working out for me? Is there something I need to change? What should I be doing right now that I'm not doing? What can I be doing better? By answering these questions, I ensure that I am on the right track and that I'm taking responsibility for what is happening. It also gives my mind a clear slate.

If my spirit gives me signals that something is out of sync, taking a moment to think about what that "something" is, releases the tension and helps me to see what I can do differently to move into a better space. I cannot just move along. I need to stop and figure out what is happening and how I need to shift.

When conflict arises, and I need to have a tough conversation, reflecting can help me to think through it and approach it from a place of love in order to get a positive outcome. Being unprepared can cause me to get caught up. I may end up saying something I don't mean, not saying what I do mean, or just having an unproductive conversation overall. But in reflection, I can gain understanding and work towards the outcome I desire.

Through reflection I am able to learn important lessons about myself and my interactions with the people I love and care about. I may come to some realizations about things that I hadn't understood before. Ultimately, by reflecting, I am making a commitment to self-improvement and fostering a lifestyle where I learn from my mistakes and seek to do better.

▲ Prayer ▲

Lord, thank you for my ability to think critically. I know that in stepping back to look at things, I get a new perspective. Please help me to take the time to reflect and understand my experiences. Lord don't let me go through life just letting life happen to me. I want to be more in tune with what is going on, what I'm doing, and what I can be doing better. I want to learn and grow from each experience that you give me. I want to clear out my thoughts so that my mind can operate at its highest capacity.

God, help me to be in touch with what my spirit is trying to tell me. Let me slow down and understand what I need to do. Instead of handling conflicts blindly, show me how to think through the situation and come up with the best plan for peaceful resolve. I know that not taking the time to think and reflect might place me in situations that are not good for me.

Lord I ask that you help me to discover something new about myself each day. Let me come to the realization that I need to about myself. I pray that I will improve myself by reflecting and never stop growing. In the name of Jesus, I lift this prayer. *Amen.*

▲ Action ▲

Check-in with yourself

Do I spend time reflecting? Do I ask myself critical questions that can help me to grow? Am I writing down my thoughts and feelings regularly?

Make a choice

Today I choose to be reflective because it helps me to see how to be better.

Act on your choice

≈ Keep a journal or take time to do written reflections.

≈ Ask yourself critical questions about how you feel and what you need to do differently.

≈ Take time to think through and assess situations.

CHAPTER TWENTY-SEVEN

Be Clear About Who You Are

"Find out who you are and be that person. That's what your soul was put on this Earth to be. Find that truth, live that truth and everything else will come."
—ELLEN DEGENERES

"For you created my inmost being; you knit me together in my mother's womb. I praise you because I am fearfully and wonderfully made; your works are wonderful. I know that full well."
—PSALM 139:13-14

▲ Affirmation ▲

If I'm being honest with myself, sometimes I forget who I am. I forget that I am a child of the Most High God, the creator of all things, the one who never fails. It's not that I don't know. I simply forget. I kind of get amnesia about who God created me to be. I forget that he knew me even before I was in my mother's womb. I forget that he created me with purpose. I forget that he sent me here with everything I need inside of me. I lose touch with this reality at times. It escapes my mind.

Today I'm declaring to remember who I am at all times. In my relationships, in my friendships, in my work environment, when I am in public. No matter where I am or what I am doing, I need to be mindful of who I am. I was fearfully and wonderfully made, crafted with clear intention and in perfection. I am not a mistake. God doesn't make mistakes. My life is meaningful. I am needed here on this earth. My boldness is needed. My energy is needed. My ideas are needed. My gifts are needed.

I. AM. NEEDED.

God looks at me as royalty. The people who engage with me will treat me as such. A person of royalty wouldn't allow folks to talk down to them. A person of royalty wouldn't settle for less than what is deserved. A person of royalty wouldn't stay in bad relationships. A person of royalty wouldn't maintain friendships that lack substance. A person of royalty wouldn't stay at dead end jobs without opportunity for growth. And since I am a person of royalty, I won't either.

▲ Prayer ▲

Lord, thank you for creating me with only the best ingredients. My mentality, physicality, emotionality, spirituality, and personality at their highest forms are nothing short of a masterpiece. You definitely took your time with me Lord. You spent time sculpting me, shaping me, molding me, and perfecting me. You poured into me everything you had.

God, I ask for your forgiveness that I sometimes forget all that you did to get me here and to keep me here. Please know that it is not my intention to walk and move as though I don't know who I am. You see Lord, as I move throughout the world I can sometimes get bogged down by all the demands that society has placed on me. It gets hard to balance who you told me I am with what the world tries to make me out to be.

Today I am asking that you help me to push aside all the predisposed notions that I've picked up throughout my life and bring me back to the beginning. Purify me, oh Lord, so that I might remember who I was when you first formed me because in essence that is who I still am, who I really am. I am not what people think of me. Lord, I am who **you** say who I am. Help me to remember this daily. Keep it at the forefront of my mind. Let it be evident in every move I make, every word I speak, every thought and in the inner spaces of my being. In Jesus name I lift this prayer. *Amen.*

▲ Action ▲

Check-in with yourself

Do I hold myself in the same high vision that God holds me in? Do I move and act in alignment with the vision that God has of me?

Make a choice

Today I choose to be clear about who I am because when I remember that I am royalty, I move as such.

Act on your choice

≈ Create a personal statement about who you are.

≈ Align your treatment of yourself with the vision God holds of you.

≈ Ensure how others treat you aligns with your vision of yourself. Don't accept anything less.

CHAPTER TWENTY-EIGHT

Be Careful with Your Words

"Be careful how you are talking to yourself because you are listening."
—LISA M. HAYES

"Death and life are in the power of the tongue, and those who love it will eat its fruits."
—PROVERBS 18:21

▲ Affirmation ▲

The words that I speak are not merely words. They are magic. They have the power to move and shift things to be for me or against me. I cannot afford to use my words loosely. My words carry with them an energy that spreads like wild fire. My words can shape my thoughts. My thoughts can shape my actions. My actions can create my reality. So, I need to be careful what I say. What am I saying to myself about myself when I speak? What am I saying to myself about my life when I speak? These things are important. Life or death truly is in the power of the tongue. I will not be passive or negative with my words. When it comes to the things I want to do, "I can't" and "impossible" will not be a part of my vocabulary. Those are not the words of a powerful person who has already been chosen by God. Instead I choose to use my words to create life.

I will be mindful of what I speak. I will choose words that honor me and move me closer to my desires. Let everything that flows from my lips be a source of positivity for me and those around me. Let my words help to create and manifest the very things that I want for my life. Once I speak it, I know it can be done. Just like

God created an entire universe using his words, I can create my own universe using mine.

I will not speak down on others or use my words to hurt other people. If I can't get my point across without using hateful words, what does that say about me and my level of maturity? What does that say about how I feel about those around me? Even in a disagreement I will use tactful ways of expressing myself, especially with those I love. If I love you, my words will demonstrate that I love you. That will not halt because we don't have the same opinion, or I am experiencing frustration. Those same words that I speak to others will reflect right back onto me. Therefore, I have a duty to myself to be mindful of the words that I am using with others.

▲ Prayer ▲

Lord, I pray that you will help me to understand the power of my words. Remind me that my words are magic. In the same way that you used words to create the world I live in Lord, I know that my words have creative power too. Let me speak into existence the very things that I want knowing that if I can speak it, then it's already mine. Your word says there is life and death in the power of the tongue and I know it to be true. Let my words speak life.

God forgive me for the times that I have not been mindful of what I said. I may not always be careful with my words. But today I ask that you cleanse my tongue of negativity and passivity. In those times when I don't know the right thing to say, please give me the right words. I never want to use my words to hurt others. I don't want to be mean spirited Lord. I want to use my words for good.

Lord please help me to change my vocabulary. Eliminate anything from it that is not creating life. Remove anything that is not pleasing to you. Show me new ways to express myself. In the name of Jesus, I lift this prayer. *Amen.*

▲ Action ▲

Check-in with yourself

Am I mindful of the words I speak? Are negative and passive words a regular part of my vocabulary? Do I truly understand the power of words and what they can create in my life?

Make a choice

Today I choose to be careful with my words because they have the power to create life or death.

Act on your choice

≈ Transition from passive words like "I might" and "I think so" to "I will" and "I know."

≈ Correct yourself if you catch yourself using negative language and let the people around you hold you accountable.

≈ Watch what you say around children especially. Their young minds absorb everything.

CHAPTER TWENTY-NINE

Be Mindful of the Information You Consume

"You are the books you read, the films you watch, the music you listen to, the people you meet, the dreams you have, and the conversations you engage in. You are what you take from these."
—JACK VANEK

"Therefore, prepare your minds for action; discipline yourselves."
—1 PETER 1:13

▲ Affirmation ▲

The information that I consume, has more of an impact on me than I might think. I'm not just simply watching television, or scrolling social media, or listening to the radio, or watching the news all for fun. These things also have an impact on my mind. While entertainment is a normal part of life, it doesn't mean that I don't need to be mindful of what I'm taking in. I won't insult my intelligence by assuming that I am unable to watch, read, or hear something without emulating what I see or that everything I consume is negative. Neither is the case. However, the truth of the matter is that much of what stays with me is subconscious. That means the information surpasses my normal ability to censor, despite how intelligent I may be.

It benefits me to be selective about my choices and be aware of what kind of results it produces in my life. Am I wasting endless hours on social media when I could be building? Am I feeling anxiety because I've watched the news late at night? Am I using certain negative words as a result of listening to certain songs or acting differently after watching certain shows? I may not need to cut these things out, but I just need to be aware of it and ensure it's not impacting me negatively.

On top of keeping an eye on what I'm taking in, I must also be mindful of what I'm putting out. Once information is public, it doesn't really go away. If I have dreams and aspirations, they could be affected by the things I decide to share. My sexual life is not necessarily something I need to share with the world. A rant about my boss, coworkers, or company is not exactly smart for me to post on social media. Disagreements involving my family should not be aired out for the world to see on social media. I will be mindful of the information I'm sharing and taking in because it doesn't only impact me.

▲ Prayer ▲

Lord I thank you for the advances of media and technology. They have made me more connected to my family, friends, and the world in many ways. I'm grateful for the information and for the entertainment that I am able to receive because of it. However, I ask that you help me to balance my use of media in a way that is conducive to my well-being. Although its entertaining Lord, I know that I cannot control the way it affects me. Please don't let me overindulge to the point that is affecting me and my ability to be productive. I pray that it does not get in the way of me focusing on other, more important things.

I ask that you teach me how to be mindful of the information that I am putting out into the world, as it has an impact beyond me. Lord, I don't want to be careless in my use of media, having an attitude of "I can post whatever I want". Just because I *can* put something out there, doesn't mean I *should*. Because I have ambitions, not caring about what I put out, is not an option. It's careless and immature. Let me be selective of what I share. Let me be more aware of how it affects me as well as others. In the name of Jesus, I lift this prayer. *Amen.*

▲ Action ▲

Check-in with yourself

Am I mindful of what I watch and listen to? Do I overconsume social media, television, news and radio? Is there a healthy balance to what I am taking it? Am I careful of what I put out?

Make a choice

Today I choose to be mindful of the information I consume because it can impact my mental space.

Act on your choice

≈ Limit the time you spend on 'entertainment'. It's okay as long as it's balanced with other stuff.

≈ Take a complete break sometimes in order to focus.

≈ Be selective about what you post online.

≈ Try not to watch the news right before bed. It can be upsetting and cause you to go to sleep with anxiety.

CHAPTER THIRTY

Be Disciplined

"One act of obedience is better than one hundred sermons."
– DIETRICH BONHOEFFER

"*Like* a city that is broken into *and* without walls is a man who has no control over his spirit."
—PROVERBS 25:28

▲ Affirmation ▲

I need to maintain discipline if I want to receive the things that God has for me. I don't have the luxury of going everywhere and doing everything. Yes, I have free will, but that doesn't mean that I don't need to exercise control over myself. Whether or not I reach my goals and have the life God has for me, depends on how much I can exercise discipline in my life.

There are certain things that my spirit can only receive when it is clear of "debris". Excessive drinking, smoking, partying, careless spending, risky sexual interactions are all debris. They make it difficult for God to get through to me. When I cut these things off or refrain temporarily (fast), I free up space in my mind and spirit to hear God more clearly. God can reveal things to me about what decisions to make and what directions to pursue. It also helps me become more mentally, physically, and emotionally resilient.

It's important that I show God I can sacrifice because of my love for him and my desire for more. I must learn to rely more on God to fulfill me than these other things. In my discipline, God will know that I am ready to take on the things he has for me.

▲ Prayer ▲

Lord I thank you in advance for giving me the strength and courage to refrain from my indulgences in order to get closer to you. God, being close to you is the safest place I can be. I know that there are things you want to see happen in my life that can only come to pass if I am disciplined and obedient. My desire for your will is greater than any temporary pleasure that I could be seeking.

If it gets difficult to maintain, Lord I ask that you give me the strength to push through. What is on the other side of my obedience will always be greater Lord. Help me to fast from unhealthy things like excessive partying, drinking, smoking, and sexual activity if need be so that I can replenish my spirit. Help me not to rely solely on fasting, expecting a miracle, but instead to use it as a tool combined with my faith to produce great results.

Lord let me be disciplined enough to know when to step away from something or someone. Let me be disciplined enough to say no to my friends when I need to. I don't have to always do what everyone else is doing. If they love me, they will still be there, In the name of Jesus, I lift this prayer. *Amen.*

▲ Action ▲

Check-in with yourself

Do I practice discipline in order to get the things I want? Am I disciplined with my spending? Am I disciplined with my eating? Am I disciplined with drinking, smoking, or partying?

Make a choice

Today I choose to be disciplined because my obedience is connected to God's will for my life.

Act on your choice

≈ Decide on one thing you need to fast from in order to focus. You will be amazed at how much you get done with a little time away from certain things.

≈ Consider cutting back on excessive drinking, smoking, and partying if these are your indulgences. It's very difficult to hear God when these things are at play.

CHAPTER THIRTY-ONE

Be Transformed Through Travel

"The world is a book and those who do not travel read only one page."
—AUGUSTINE OF HIPPO

"You provide a broad path for my feet."
—PSALM 18:36

▲ Affirmation ▲

If God created the entire world in all its beauty for me to see, why would I confine myself just to where I live? There is an entire world out there for me to see. Seven continents, 195 countries, and thousands of islands. All of this was made from God's imagination. It was made for my enjoyment. Being in the same place creates a habitual and predictable conscience. It's difficult for me to gain new perspective this way. My mind operates based on what it sees and takes in. If I am only taking in the same thing, I am not nourishing my mind in a new way.

Travel isn't just about the beauty or about posting dope pictures on Instagram, Facebook, or Snapchat, although that's cool too. A picture on IG of me in front of the Eiffel Tower would be dope. A picture on Facebook of me swimming with the dolphins in Aruba would be dope. A video of me on Snapchat riding 4—wheelers through the deserts of Dubai would be dope. But that's not all there is. When I travel, I am expanding my mind. I am seeing new images, experiencing new cultures and hearing new languages. I am widening my curiosity and awareness. There is transformation in traveling. I begin to think a little differently. I come to know myself a little better. There is something about being in a new place, something about unplugging from it all, something about surrounding myself with different people that awakens my soul just a bit more. It gives me a different sense of freedom. I bring back with me a new perspective each time, that makes life that much more meaningful.

Traveling solo is a different level of the traveling game. There is nothing that says I trust myself and love being with myself more than my willingness to take a trip alone. I will get to learn more about myself. What do I like to do when no one else has a say? What do I care about when no one else has a say? What would I try if no one else had a say? I will be able to do whatever I want, whenever I want and however I want. I will be able to push myself outside of my comfort zone and gain a different type of confidence. There is just something liberating about it! It's a rare form of fulfillment with self.

So, I am not going to be afraid to get out there and see the world God has created. I am going to see as much of it as I can in my time here. Through my travels, I will become more cultured, more aware of myself, and more fulfilled.

▲ Prayer ▲

Lord, thank you for creating such a beautiful world for me to see. You did not hold back when you began forming the oceans and mountains that produced such beautiful islands and countries. Remind me Lord, that traveling is not just about having fun and taking photos. Every place has a culture and a rich story behind it. It is one that I get to be a part. You gifted us with these different languages and cultures so that we would have new experiences. I thank you for the diversity and imagination.

God, I don't want to be confined to just the place I live. Help me to not be afraid to go out and explore the world you have set before me, even if it's alone. Remind me that when I travel alone, your protection and presence is always with me, so I need not be afraid. I can rest assured that you will be with me.

As I travel Lord, open my mind up to new possibilities. Help me to learn new things. Send me great people and experiences on the journey. Let the energy and spirit of each place transform my mind and awaken my soul. In the name of Jesus, I lift this prayer. *Amen.*

▲ Action ▲

Check-in with yourself

How often am I traveling? When I travel, do I take in the culture around me? Have I traveled alone? Am I afraid to do so? Where is a place that I have always wanted to go? Why haven't I been there yet?

Make a choice

Today I choose to be transformed through travel because there is so much beauty God created for me to see.

Act on your choice

≈ Go to a place you've always wanted to visit.

≈ Budget and plan in advance so you can enjoy the activities that you like.

≈ Travel solo at least once in your life so you can experience yourself in a new way.

PART VI

• • •

What to Keep

CHAPTER THIRTY-TWO

Keep the Right People in Your Circle

"Surround yourself with only people who are going to lift you higher. "
—OPRAH WINFREY

"Do not be deceived: Bad company corrupts good morals."
—1 CORINTHIANS 15:33

▲ Affirmation ▲

The people I surround myself with play a huge role in shaping my present and future. I cannot afford not to be concerned with who I keep in my circle. Who is in my circle has just as much impact on my goals as I do. There might be friends that I've had for a long time, but if they are not conducive to the place I'm trying to go, then it's time for me to level up. There could even be family members who are causing me more harm than good. I won't cut them off out of love, but it doesn't mean they have to be in my circle.

The people who are using and abusing me have to go. The toxic people who drain my energy have to go. The people who can't seem to understand how to respect me and treat me with the care and concern I deserve, have to go. I know that it is not a personal judgment on them. It is simply a matter of what is good for me given the goals and vision that I have.

It's not only about making sure I'm not around the wrong people. It's also about making sure I am around the right people. In order to reach my goals, I have to align myself with people who are going in the same direction— forward. There are people with skills, talents and connections that I need to be around. Not so I can use them but so that we can exchange and build together.

▲ Prayer ▲

Lord, I pray that you will help me to discern the types of individuals that I need to keep in my presence. If there are folks who don't mean me well and aren't a part of your plans for me, Lord I ask you to remove them. If there are folks who can't seem to want to do better, God distance me from them. I'm not better than anyone God, but I can make better choices. Lord, I know that who I spend my time with plays a significant role in whether I can achieve the call you have on my life. Let me examine the people close to me. Help me to make the difficult choice when I need to let folks go or alter my relationship.

Most importantly God, I ask that you bring into my life people who will bring goodness to my spirit and my space. Please connect me with dreamers and doers. Connect me with resourceful people who are not afraid to get things done. Lord, I need friends with bold faith, friends who are not afraid to stand for me, friends who I can pray with and pray for. Make my top 5 your top 5 Lord. Whoever you have for me God, that is who I want to be in my circle. I trust that you know what is best for me and you are able to see things I cannot see. Show me how to keep a circle aligned to your will. In the name of Jesus, I lift this prayer. *Amen.*

▲ Action ▲

Check-in with yourself

Who's in my circle? Are they helping me or hurting me? Am I growing because of the people in my circle? Are they supportive? What kind of character do they have? How does being around them affect me?

Make a choice

Today I choose to keep the right people in my circle because who I allow in my life determines if my dreams come to pass.

Act on your choice

≈ Drop the 'no new friends' mentality. You can keep your old friends, if they are good for you, and still make new friends who possess the characteristics you admire. It's tough to grow around the same people all the time.

≈ If there is someone in your circle who is causing you more harm than good, you might want to consider a change.

CHAPTER THIRTY-THREE

Keep Your Long-term Goals in Mind

"You can't build a long-term future on short term thinking."
—BILLY COX

"No, Christian brothers, I do not have that life yet. But I do one thing. I forget everything that is behind me and look forward to that which is ahead of me. My eyes are on the crown. I want to win the race and get the crown of God's call from heaven through Christ Jesus."
—PHILIPPIANS 3:13-14

▲ Affirmation ▲

Everything that I am building is for a greater purpose. I am working towards a long-term vision. There are things that I am doing now that may not bear fruit right away, but I will not get discouraged. It is a part of the process. When things are not showing up right away, I must keep my eyes on the prize and press towards the mark. I just need to keep the end goal in mind and ask myself what am I fighting for, what am I trying to accomplish here?

Knowing what I am working towards, gives me the fuel I need to push through. It also gives me a clear vision to follow. Through this, I can quickly discern if something will fit in with my vision or not so that I can begin to align my decisions and plans with the long-term vision that I have for my life.

The things that I strive towards are not overnight wins. They require me to be in it for the long haul. Short-term thinking will not get me to a long-term outcome. I cannot focus on how to get something quickly when I am working to build a legacy. It's going to take a lot but it's also going to create a lot. What I'm working to leave behind is something far greater than me.

▲ Prayer ▲

Lord, I pray that you will keep my mind focused on the end goal. My long-term vision requires a lot of me and I pray that you will give me the strength to see it through to the end. God, my goal is to win the race even if the finish line is far out. Push me to strive towards it, even if I cannot see it from where I am.

I trust that your promises for me will come to pass no matter how difficult it gets. Help me to keep building even through the tough times. Remind me that it gets greater later and that everything I am doing now will pay off. Every brick I lay will have a purpose in the end. So, what may seem like a small step has its place too.

God, don't let me get blinded by the desire for a *right now* victory. The small wins are great, they matter too. But I ask that you keep my mind and my eyes focused on the bigger picture. There may be some things that look good in the short term that will not serve me in the long-term. I pray that you will help me to discern these things. In the name of Jesus, I lift this prayer. *Amen.*

▲ Action ▲

Check-in with yourself

Do I make decisions based on short-term outcomes or long-term outcomes? Am I planning ahead and sowing seeds for the things I want in the future? How can what I am doing now fit into the legacy I want to leave behind?

Make a choice

Today I choose to keep my long-term goals in mind because it will help me to put my decisions and efforts in their proper perspective.

Act on your choice

≈ Do long-term planning. Write down your 5-year, 10-year, and 20-year goals.

≈ Take small steps toward a big future. Everything doesn't have to be a big leap, work towards longevity.

CHAPTER THIRTY-FOUR

Keep Aiming for Excellence

"We are what we repeatedly do. Excellence, then, is not an act, but a habit."
—ARISTOTLE

"Show yourself in all respects to be a model of good works, and in your teaching show integrity, dignity, and sound speech."
—TITUS 2:7-8

▲ Affirmation ▲

There is nothing mediocre about me. Everything I do, I do it in excellence. No 'half steppin'. I set the bar high and use all that God has placed within me to reach that bar. Going for the easy wins is not going to cut it. I won't be stretched that way. I won't be able to test out my full power that way. I won't be able to use all my talent that way. It is in my pursuit of excellence that I am able to show my distinction and my brilliance, and use all this greatness God placed inside of me.

I want to be able to see myself at my best. I want those I love and care about to see me at my best too. Not the me who *almost* did it, the me who tried or the me who made it half way. No, I need them to see me when I am operating in excellence. This doesn't mean that I will be perfect or won't make mistakes but that I am aiming to do my best. If I'm not going to try to do my best, I might as well not try at all. What can I gain from a mediocre effort? There is no learning in mediocrity. There is no growth in mediocrity. There is no power in mediocrity. The truth is that anything less than excellence is a waste of my talent. It's an insult to the brilliance that God created in me.

I'm not going to settle for less. I won't settle for a quarter, a half, not even 99.9%. I am going to go after it all. I want all God has for me. I want the wins that no one else wanted parts of because they couldn't see the glory in it. I want the wins that no one else wanted to fight for because it looked like too much work. I want the wins that come after the failures. I want the wins that I have to share with others. I want the wins that don't get public recognition. I want the wins that require my blood, sweat, and tears. In my excellence, God will make all of this work for my good.

▲ Prayer ▲

Lord, you never cease to amaze me. I am awestruck by the spirit of excellence in everything you do. Thank you for setting a high standard for what you expect of me. God, I know without a doubt that you have equipped me with power unimaginable. I know that you have given me strength to weather any storm. I know that you have given me a mind sharp enough to figure anything out. Help me to use these tools Lord, as I pursue excellence. When I don't want to set the bar high for myself Lord, set it high for me. Raise it up and show me that I have everything in me to meet and exceed the expectations. Don't give me a pass Lord when I try to be less than what I can be, do less than what I can do or give less than what I can give.

Push me to be only my best. In the process Lord, show me new parts of me that I didn't even know I had. Lord, I am not on a quest for perfection. I am on a quest for excellence. I am seeking excellence because I want to use all of the talent you have given me. I want to be the best to myself and those around me Lord. Let my walk be excellent Lord, let my talk be excellent, let my thoughts be excellent, let every move be made in excellence.

Let me not settle into mediocrity. Let me not water down my dreams and hopes in exchange for comfort. Lord, push me to my full capacity. I am standing on the edge of greatness. Bring me down right into it. Where the best of me lives, that's where I want to be Lord. I want to be *fully* in your will. Don't let me half step. Don't let me give out when people say no. Let me not be burdened by the difficulty at the end. Instead, push me past the Nos. Push me past the trying times Lord. In the name of Jesus, I lift this prayer. ***Amen.***

▲ Action ▲

Check-in with yourself

Do I set the bar high when it comes to the things I want to achieve? Am I aiming to do my best or the minimum? Do I often feel like I've done enough or like I could do better? Am I truly pursuing excellence in all that I do?

Make a choice

Today I choose to keep aiming for excellence because I am capable of greatness and I won't settle for mediocrity.

Act on your choice

≈ If you feel that you're doing well, try to be even better. Don't stop aiming higher just because you've accomplished things.

≈ Go for something you feel is out of your league. And if you don't feel prepared for the high-level opportunity you want, get prepared!

CHAPTER THIRTY-FIVE

Keep God First

"If you have not chosen the kingdom of God first, it will in the end make no difference what you have chosen instead."
— WILLIAM LAW

"But seek ye first the kingdom of God, and his righteousness; and all these things shall be added unto you."
—MATTHEW 6:33

▲ Affirmation ▲

If I even think for a moment that I can do this thing called Life without God, I am sadly mistaken. I would have never made it this far without God. Everything I have, everything I am, everything I've done has been blessed by God. There are an infinite number of things that God has done on my behalf that I'll never even know about. Battles he has fought, roadblocks he's moved from my path, plots against me that he has turned into wins. I would never even have enough time to wrap my mind around all that God has done and continues to do.

Putting God first gives honor to the many blessings that he has given me and deepens my relationship with God. This is not about religion. It's not about someone telling me how to be in relationship with God, how to worship God, or what God will and won't do to me if I don't follow his orders. I put God first for one reason only: because he deserves it! Honestly, if I can't give honor to the one who created me and puts breath in my lungs, then how can I honor myself or anyone else for that matter?

When I put God first, I put me first. If God holds my life in his hands, then spending time with him is a no brainer. It's like life support. I can put God first in whichever way I choose. It can be by attending church, by spending alone time in communication with God through prayer, through praise and worship or by reading the Bible. Whatever the method is, I need to make sure that God knows I appreciate what he's done, and I understand what he expects of me. I am seeking his guidance for this journey called life so that I may do his works and do them well.

It is not just directly through prayer, worship, praise, and studying the word that I honor God, but also through how I live and move. I need to move like I am serving God. Folks need to be able to see the God in me. They need to see it in my actions and my words. I don't have to be in a church to show my honor for God, I can show it wherever I am, just by who I am.

▲ Prayer ▲

Lord, thank you for the endless mercy you have shown unto me. I have the utmost reverence for all that you do. Even if I had a thousand tongues I could never say thank you enough. You protect me, provide for me, and keep me day in and day out. Your works are seen and unseen, known and unknown. Sometimes I don't know how you do it all Lord, but with every blessing you show your love for me. There is no way that I can do this thing called life without you and I would never want to.

God, please forgive me if I haven't put you first 100% of the time. Please forgive me for allowing other things to take center stage ahead of you. You always deserve to be first. Nothing should ever come before you given all that you do.

I pray to always remain close to you. In connection with you is where I find the peace, joy, and happiness that I could never gain from this world. I am glad that I can be connected to you in the ways that work for me. Our relationship is not dependent on a particular place. Having the relationship and honoring you is what matters most. In the name of Jesus, I lift this prayer. *Amen.*

▲ Action ▲

Check-in with yourself

Am I giving God the place he deserves in my life? How am I demonstrating to God that he comes first? What does my relationship with God look like and how can it be better?

Make a choice

Today I choose to keep God first because he deserves it.

Act on your choice

≈ Pray daily. Communicating with God is the best way to express your gratitude for all he does for you and to ask him for what you need.

≈ Understand what God expects of you by reading the word and try your best to uphold those standards.

≈ Attend church; or worship in any way you see fit.

CHAPTER THIRTY-SIX

Keep Developing Yourself

"If you are under the impression you have already perfected yourself, you will never rise to the heights you are no doubt capable of."
—KAZUO ISHIGURO

"Do not conform to the pattern of this world, but be transformed by the renewing of your mind. Then you will be able to test and approve what God's will is—his good, pleasing and perfect will."
—ROMANS 12:2

▲ Affirmation ▲

If I don't continue to develop myself, I cannot grow and learn. My mind is like a muscle, and when I don't develop it, I keep it at a certain limit. It needs constant development in order to operate at its full capacity. God needs me to be fully operating in order to be able to do his will. The things he is expecting of me will require me to be my best self.

I want to rise to the highest heights possible. That means I need to continue to grow. In the renewing of my mind is where I find my greatest potential. Being in a continuous state of development keeps me prepared for the opportunities that will arrive.

If I have a business idea, I don't have to be an expert on all the things related to my idea. I can develop myself in the areas I need to, in order to succeed. As I move further in my journey, I need to upgrade my knowledge too.

There can never be enough knowledge, understanding, and perspective to be obtained. Even if I feel that I'm already educated, I can still learn a new skill in order to continue developing myself. My attitude is "the more I learn, the better off I will be".

▲ Prayer ▲

Lord I pray that you help me to continue to develop myself mentally and spiritually. Show me the areas of my life that I need to improve. I want to continue to grow and develop in order to reach my goals and become a better me.

God, I know that I cannot achieve the great things you have for me if I remain the same. I cannot reach the heights you have set for me if I am underdeveloped. When opportunities come, they will pass me by if I am not prepared. Please give me the endurance to continue seeking new knowledge always.

Lord, don't let me get complacent; thinking that I know all there is to know. There is always an area that I can grow in. Even in my old age, there will always be something for me to learn. There is no stopping point for self-development.

When I work on myself, it doesn't only benefit me but everyone around me. I pray that you will mold and shape me into my best self. In the name of Jesus, I lift this prayer. *Amen.*

▲ Action ▲

Check-in with yourself

Am I often seeking new ways to develop myself? When was the last time I read a book or article? Are there things I need to gain new skills in?

Make a choice

Today I choose to keep developing myself because being my best self helps me to be prepared for what God has for me.

Act on your choice

≈ Read often. There are millions of books on every topic imaginable. Keep your mind nourished!

≈ Attend events with business-minded people.

≈ Take a class or go back to school for a higher degree if it fits in with your career plans.

CHAPTER THIRTY-SEVEN

Keep Money in its Proper Perspective

"Focusing your life solely on making a buck shows a certain poverty of ambition. It asks too little of yourself. Because it's only when you hitch your wagon to something larger than yourself, that you realize your true potential."
—BARACK OBAMA

"No one can serve two masters. Either you will hate the one and love the other, or you will be devoted to the one and despise the other. You cannot serve both God and money."
—MATTHEW 6:24

▲ Affirmation ▲

They say "money makes the world go round", but it doesn't make *my* world go round. Although there are aspects of my life that can be disrupted if I don't keep my finances in order, my peace is not dependent on the possession of money. My peace as it relates to money has to do with understanding where finances fit into my overall vision for my life. Many of the things I want to accomplish will require me to have access to finances. In order to achieve my dreams, I may need to take a class, buy a book, attend an event or workshop, pay for a business license, etc. These are all things that can help me to progress in life and lay a financial foundation that can be passed down for generations.

If I'm spending money on things I don't need, not tracking my spending, or not prioritizing my funds for things that really matter, what am I saying to God about my ability to handle what he has already blessed me with? And would he trust me with more? Even if I feel that I don't earn enough, I still have a responsibility to spend wisely. If my current finances do not align with my needs, I am fully capable of pursuing and developing other opportunities for myself. The struggle may be real but it doesn't have to be a way of life. If I'm willing to work for it, I can have the financial freedom that I want. It's not okay if I can't afford basic needs like food, clothing, and shelter. It's not okay if I can't afford to visit the doctor and make sure I'm healthy. It's not okay if I can't afford to handle an emergency should it arise. It's not okay if I can't afford to go on vacation and celebrate my hard work. I have to create a situation where I can afford to survive and do the things that make me happy, not choose between the two.

Although I don't want to struggle, money can never be my sole purpose for what I do. Focusing on money to this extent is a sure way to lose sight of Gods' real vision for my life. What I possess is simply a byproduct of my work used to fulfill God's purpose. It is not an end goal by itself.

Chasing money will never get me anywhere and being selfish with it won't either. I need to remember that all I have comes from God. Creating a financial situation where I can thrive and not just survive is not only important for my personal gain, but also so that I can have enough to give to those in need. As long as I am not suffering, giving to others should be a given.

▲ Prayer ▲

Lord, thank you for blessing me with the finances that I have. No amount is too little to be thankful for. I pray that you will continue to bless me with the things I need while helping me to grow financially. Your word says that you have plans to prosper me Lord and I want to see those plans come to pass.

God, I ask that you help me to be intentional with my spending. Remove from me the need to spend money on things that only serve the purpose of impressing others. I want to be faithful with my funds Lord. God, I pray to be able to create a strong financial foundation that can be passed down for generations.

Please show me how to handle my finances in a way that is pleasing to you. I know that being prosperous is not about having money just for the sake of it but for fulfilling a higher purpose. I pray that you will keep me centered on that higher purpose. Let me be a giver when I can and create a lifestyle that allows me to give to others. Remind me that I cannot receive with a closed hand. In the name of Jesus, I lift this prayer. *Amen.*

▲ Action ▲

Check-in with yourself

What's my viewpoint on money? Is it a means to an end for me, or the end? Am I chasing money? Do I feel like I have enough to thrive and not just survive? Do I have enough to be able to give back?

Make a choice

Today I choose to keep money in its proper perspective because chasing money will get me nowhere.

Act on your choice

≈ Create a budget and stick to it. Tell your money where to go before it spends itself.

≈ Check your credit often and work to maintain a high score.

≈ Set goals for how much income you need to have a lifestyle of financial freedom.

PART VII

...

What to Own

CHAPTER THIRTY-EIGHT

Own Your Truth

"There is no greater agony than bearing an untold story inside you."
—MAYA ANGELOU

"Then you will know the truth, and the truth will set you free."
—JOHN 8:32

▲ Affirmation ▲

When I'm not walking in my truth, I create a blockage between me and the things I want. Being true to myself means that I accept me as I am despite any past circumstances I may have endured. There may be some tough things about my truth that I have to deal with. But there is nothing to be afraid of. The truth can't hurt me, it can only free me. My history, even the dark parts of me are nothing to be ashamed. I don't have to be a victim to my past. I can choose to write my own story and be the victor.

Although there are other people connected to my truth, owning my truth is about me and not them. I am not looking to blame anyone nor give anyone credit. I simply want to be clear about what has shaped me and how that impacts me now, whether good or bad. This will take some vulnerability on my part because I know that walking in my truth won't make everyone happy and it will require me to make some difficult choices. But if the price is my freedom, I cannot sit back and not walk in my truth, or own only part of it. No, I will accept it all because my freedom means that much to me.

In exploring my truth without any blame or fault, I can find compassion for those who are connected to me, those who shaped me and impacted me. I can find understanding. I can find acceptance. I can find healing. I can find forgiveness. I can find trust. **I can find me.** Me: before the world told me who I was. Me: before life beat against me. Me: before people had an opinion of me. Just me: the way God made me. Pure, whole, and perfect. That's the truth about me.

▲ Prayer ▲

Lord the truth can sometimes feel like a burden to bear. There is a part of me who would rather not explore my full truth. You know Lord that it ain't all pretty. It takes courage and strength to choose the truth. The courage to accept that no matter what my truth holds, it's all a part of me and the strength to fight back the desire to run away from it. But God I know that my truth is connected to my freedom. Remind me oh Lord that there is nothing to fear. I am the dawn and the dark, I do not have to be afraid of myself.

You already know every part of me and yet each step of the way you've continued to see only the best in me. I ask that you remove any sense of shame, guilt, regret, or fears that may stop me from owning my truth. I thank you for showing me a vision of myself in the way that you see me: pure, whole, and perfect; lacking nothing. Please help me to have compassion, understanding, and forgiveness for anyone connected to a hurtful part of my story. I pray that through my truth, I will get healing. Make me the victor and not the victim, Lord. Help me to own my truth so that I can get free and stay free. In the name of Jesus, I lift this prayer. *Amen.*

▲ Action ▲

Check-in with yourself

What part of my truth am I afraid to own? What dark parts do I need to come to grips with? How would owning my truth improve my well-being?

Make a choice

Today I choose to own my truth because there is power and healing in my story.

Act on your choice

≈ Speak your truth unapologetically. Don't be afraid of what someone else will feel. Owning your life's story will set you free.

≈ Write down the parts of your truth you struggle with and ask God to help you accept them.

CHAPTER THIRTY-NINE

Own Your Role

"When you think everything is someone else's fault, you will suffer a lot. When you realize that everything springs only from yourself, you will learn both peace and joy."
—14th DALAI LAMA

"Whoever conceals his transgressions will not prosper, but he who confesses and forsakes them will obtain mercy."
—PROVERBS 28:13

▲ Affirmation ▲

No one else is in charge of my life and my happiness. The peace that I want can only be created when I take ownership over the life that I want. In order to see my true vision manifest, I must take responsibility for what I am, for what I do, and for what I want. I cannot sit idle and expect that things will just come to me. I cannot wait for people to do things on my behalf, not even God. It's no doubt that God has power over my life, but God and I are in a partnership. This partnership comes with responsibility on my part. There are things that I have to take accountability for. What I decide to do with my time and my gifts is not on God. Who I choose to allow into my life is not on God. Whether or not I decide to operate in my full authority is not on God. Those things are up to me. God gives me direction, strength, resources, ideas, power, confidence. He gives me a lot, more than enough of what I need. But what I do with those tools is up to me. What makes my relationship with God so beautiful is that I have free will. Every great relationship is built on two core principles: freedom and choice. It's no different in my relationship with God.

Response — Ability. Whether or not I have the desires of my heart is based on my ability to respond. I know that I cannot control everything, but I can choose how I respond to the people, situations, and opportunities that are placed in my path. That is how I use my own power. That is how I create my own peace. I'm not going to walk through life waiting for things to happen to me, blaming others for the life that I am living, or putting all the responsibility onto God. I am going to move as though I have power. I will take responsibility for who I am being, what I am doing, and whether or not I have the things that I want. Taking responsibility opens up a window of freedom that deepens my sense of power. I can use that power to get the results that I want.

▲ Prayer ▲

Lord, thank you for doing exceedingly and abundantly more than I could ever hope, dream, or imagine. In this partnership, God, you never fail to do your part. There are even times when you do *my* part, when you stand in the gap, when you make whole what I can only offer in pieces. I know that you have great expectations of me, because you know who you made me to be. You know my strength better than I do, you know my abilities better than I do, and you know my desires better than I do. That is why you expect so much of me.

Thanks for not ever letting me settle and get away with not taking responsibility. Who would I be if I were not accountable to you? Or if you allowed me to continue pointing the finger at everyone else never taking a step back to look in the mirror? Or let my inner most desires just fade away? I'm thankful that you never let it happen. Even when I make excuses and try to escape from doing what you called me to do and who you called me to be, you step in and remind me that you made me for more. Help me to have the maturity to accept responsibility for everything that manifests in my life, good and bad. Continue to hold me accountable oh Lord. In the name of Jesus, I lift this prayer. *Amen.*

▲ Action ▲

Check-in with yourself

Do I take responsibility for my life and the things that happen in it? Am I always blaming someone else? Do I approach things from a victim standpoint or a victor standpoint?

Make a choice

Today I choose to own my role because I am responsible for my life.

Act on your choice

≈ Drop the victim story. The power is in the victory. Be sure to own your story in a way that makes you the victor and not the victim.

≈ Take responsibility for any part you play in a situation without needing to focus on the role of other people.

CHAPTER FORTY

Own Your Thoughts

"Your mind is like your bed, you have to make it up every day and be careful who you let in."
—UNKNOWN

"Keep awake! Do not sleep like others. Watch and keep your minds awake to what is happening."
—1 THESSALONIANS 5:6

▲ Affirmation ▲

There are many things that may run through my mind at a given moment, but those thoughts do not represent me. They are simply an inward reflection of the influences around me, some past and some present, some good and some bad. It's important that I don't get wrapped up in my thoughts because of the anxiety and negative disposition that it can create.

I. AM. NOT. MY. THOUGHTS.

By being more aware of my thoughts, I regain the power to decide what to do with them. I can determine which thoughts should be acted on and which shouldn't so that I am not acting on impulse. Because much of my thinking is subconscious, the negative thoughts can sometimes seep in unnoticed and if not checked I can end up in a bad mood or doing something that is not healthy for me.

I declare to take back power over my thoughts. My ability to discern healthy thoughts from unhealthy thoughts will grow stronger as I pay close attention to them. I will not let them run me instead I will remain in control.

▲ Prayer ▲

Lord thank you for this mind you have given me. It is no doubt a brilliant masterpiece. But sometimes the constant thoughts can overtake me. God, there are aspects of my thinking that have been shaped by the world I live in which is not always a healthy place. I ask that you help me to maintain control over this. I don't want my mind to be made up by the things that have happened to me. I want to be able to decide for myself what makes sense. I know that my thoughts turn into actions, so I ask Lord that you help me to guard my thoughts.

Lord, sometimes I can over think things. Please help me to see that many of the problems I think I have, are all in my head. Show me that things actually only have as much power as my mind allows them to. Let me not allow things to spiral out of control because I am thinking of the worse when I am capable of doing the best.

Give me the ability to quickly discern negative thoughts from positive ones. If I begin to allow the negative thoughts to overtake me Lord, please step in and shift my thinking. Help me to gain greater control of my mind, so that I can reap the benefit of all it has to offer. In the name of Jesus, I lift this prayer. *Amen.*

▲ Action ▲

Check-in with yourself

Do I feel in control of my thoughts or does my mind sometimes take over? Do I usually process things or just let them happen? How can I have more control over my thoughts and make sure they are healthy?

Make a choice

Today I choose to own my thoughts because I have the power to control my mind.

Act on your choice

≈ Try to separate yourself from your thoughts. Know that they don't all come from you but rather from the influences around you. This will help you to better understand the things that come to your mind. Once you are aware, you can have better control.

≈ Let go of any negative beliefs you have about yourself and others.

Dear Reader,

Thank You for reading *Inner Peace is the New Success!* It is my prayer that through this book you've gained the clarity needed to begin creating a life of peace. I wish you much success on the journey ahead!

Visit my Website or Social Media for:
- Inspirational messages
- Resources
- Events
- Other updates

And spread the word! If you know someone who could benefit from this book, feel free to buy a copy as a gift or share information on where to purchase.

With Gratitude,

DaVida

Acknowledgments

To my sister, LaMeeka: My heart is never empty because of the love we share. We have been each other's rock through every trial. God had a purpose for us despite it all. There is not a thing in the world that I wouldn't do for you. I love you immensely and I am honored to be your sister.

To Aunt Tina: I am eternally grateful for the sacrifices you made for me. The unspeakable courage and strength it took for you to step up and raise me is honorable to say the least. There is a special place in God's heart for you and there is a special place in mine too. I love you always.

To Theresa: You took me in as your own daughter. You've been there for me in every season. You never hesitate to give me your love and support. I am a better woman because of you, and I continue to be inspired by the big heart you have. I love and cherish you deeply!

To Shana: Your kindness and thoughtfulness are just a few of the things that make you one of the most amazing women I know. It's hard to put into words how much of a blessing it is to know you. You have a heart of gold. Thank you for being a shining example of what it is to be a great person. You make God proud!

To Takeema: Having you as best friend has made my life that much more meaningful. You are truly a gift. I appreciate the advice, encouragement, and support you have given me through the years. Just your presence in my life is a blessing. I value and love you dearly.

Made in the USA
Columbia, SC
26 May 2018